ESKIMO DIARY

Thomas Frederiksen

ESKIMO DIARY

Foreword by Emil Rosing
English translation by Jack Jensen and Val Clery
Caligraphy by Mel Poteck

PELHAM BOOKS · LONDON

First published in Denmark, under the title
Gronlandske Dagbogsblade, by Gyldendal,
Copenhagen, 1980

This edition published in Great Britain by
Pelham Books Ltd
44 Bedford Square
London
WC1B 3DU
1981

Originally translated from Greenlandic into
Danish by Emil Rosing
Translated from the Danish edition by Jack Jensen
English text by Val Clery

ISBN 0 7207 1311 0

An international co-production arranged by
Gyldendal, Copenhagen

Printed in Portugal

Foreword

Thomas Frederiksen was born in Igíniarfik in 1939. His forefathers on both sides were famed in their district as great hunters. At that time, the whole basis of life was hunting, which was governed by various unwritten laws. Hunters alternated between hunting districts in order not to over-hunt in any one place.

Thomas and his brothers were brought up as hunters and have always been involved in fishing. Today, techniques and modern civilisation have become such decisive factors in daily life that the risk of over-hunting has increased, because, among other things, the importance of distance has lessened. And in Greenland we see over and over again how human influence on nature disturbs its rhythm.

In the old days, Greenland society was static and no great changes in culture or trade occurred. Experience was passed from generation to generation through accounts and stories of everyday life, cultural life being reinforced as a result. The art of story-telling was enriching and educational, giving colour to everyday life.

Art was very much a part of daily life; the decoration of household articles and hunting equipment, the carving of sculptures, patterns in clothing and the decorations of the women's leatherwork all added pleasure to everyday living.

Since early youth, Thomas has kept a diary for his own amusement, noting down events and experiences of his own as well as those told him by others. He appreciates Greenland humour and delights in the use of genuine Greenland expressions. Sometimes he shows his pride of and respect for his forefathers by reviving tales and legends, at the same time, describing developments and their consequences. He considers it important to be concerned with future development so that it is guided to the benefit of the community.

Two years ago, I discovered that Thomas had handed his diary to *Grafisk Vaerksted* (Graphic Workshop) in Godthåb (Nûk) with the remark: 'Hope you will enjoy it and find inspiration and pleasure from it.'

The contents are a small social and cultural history in pictures and text. Like his forefathers, Thomas has drawn his greatest inspiration from the sea.

My thanks to Thomas for his co-operation in making his diary available to a great many people.

March 1980
Emil Rosing

6

Kânâk

Upernavik

Ûmának

Kekertarssuak · · Ilulissat
Ausiait · · Kâsigiánguit

Sisimiut

Manîtsok ·

Nûk

Pâmiut ·

Ivigtût ·
Kakortok ·

Iqdlorrortût ·

Angmagssalik ·

My First Illustration In Colour

When I was only 15 years old, this is how it used to look whenever a hunter came back from the hunt in the Northlands.

It was always exciting when my father brought home a seal. My mother would skin it and would share the meat with everybody in our hamlet.

Sharing the catch from the hunt is a local tradition, and it always made us happy to see the pleasure of neighbours, especially those who were poor and had children, when they got their share.

umingara, suyugdluse

15. ni nik   ukiorcardluga amerpara tássa kumugseu A
vangnámok tikíton   pisarnorput na-
gorkuturalugo. ila nuámertawaon atáita pisakuvumao.
dluni tikikáiga mo

nokáilo awámap pu-   _Thomas Frederiksen_

lagtaryia, nunawacatimitello pajugdluui ruáinu-
tawaon, sealungmik piigssiluisuk. nümoutdlo
nuánaarmurat nuánugumningtoince ayomang-
tagut uucuardlugit. pisaca toearáiga rude i no bu
matut pajugterlapuit. uayona tawnitdlon.

This is another memory from about the same time. It shows a great lake in the North, where I have only been once, but where our people have always gone to camp and hunt reindeer as long as anyone can remember.

As the picture shows, the hunters have just brought in a reindeer buck. It is said that in those days, anyone, man or woman, was strong enough to carry a whole reindeer.

"áma táuna 15 nunk ukioxardlunga áisuliagaráxa, Nagsugtúg. Auserssuane ávaxal aléingerme temáxsimáxtut saxuáxu kangxane imá dóssagôx xáxa Auglexaxagxytex.

táuna áma tuleordlugáinarmik amingaráxa dxkuiksiarsimasara naxoxxeulaxaluga.

xlnoxta pangxxexsuax lileixxsmaxvä xluxgtúxitxdluga táuna xujuligut makuxsimatigâl ilaxegox áma arnat paxxgmerit xluxngaisa, likxuxtax pait nangmagdlugit.

Thomas Frederiksen

This is an imaginary scene I painted many years ago. It shows kayaks and a skin-covered women's boat during a whale hunt. Traditionally, only men took part in the whale hunt, but in some places in the old days women, dressed in their parkas, were used to row the boats.

Special names are given to each stage of the whale hunt. This shows a whale being harpooned at the Anguvigartorfik, or Place of Harpooning. Seal bladders are attached to the harpoon to prevent the whale from escaping. When a whale does escape and goes aground, that is called the Altu, or The Touching. And wherever the whale is finally killed is called the Arfiorfik, or The Whale Hunt Place.

3.

uma tássa taksordliungarnak 1955-me amingara
arfangniat umiat kainaldlo angutainarssui-
ñor arfangniartaranuk? Sinmianili amat lugtut
umunå atia tássa Anguvingarfiup avatáne arfer
kainap umiatdlo suyrgtuata avatardaliuåt eg-
to agtormago ama atsrugssimavåt Avigner-
niap avatãni Sotagfingme pisaussimavåt.
Arferssiorfiagmuk mialrssulransiq-
ko (tauvane ama kaliralucarfiqpaussuakarpox)
A.Aartussen Thomas Frederiksen
Igmuiarfru

This picture shows a group of walruses afloat on an ice pack along the Western shore. In the old days, when walruses were plentiful, this was a very common sight.

Here, with the sun sinking in the West, a group of walruses aboard their icy boat float in towards the shore.

4.

ât͡ſiǫ kôʼsimassut ſauʼnâ ʼãma (ſakordlôrdlugo
summerpoκ κaŋa aɔtſit ſiκſarsimasarataͣllar-
mâʼla sumuʼnur leitôuut taʼvilurssor puʼtâvat ru-
nanuʼt ſalilursson. (imaʼua κeuʼurkarssuͥp κarrutu-
ŋâni) Thulumiʼlûnut valiuſiuga auʼuʼguʼatacao sikorhuarni ora-
lardlugit   Γ. Kruʼuʼaſ

ͣma ſauʼuaʼne ſkaʼuʼurssuakarsimaʼgame ruʼurtas-
ssuͥp aʼvatâne urʼuâ ʼsârugaʼluʼuaʼusumile. kaliʼuʼuaʼgdlutͣllo i-
lait aʼgisuʼijuʼuʼut sâtugʼsaʼtaʼlsʼilai aʼgiuʼiſuʼjuʼut muʼurutuʼquʼor
ſuʼxanuʼuͣt ſiaʼsuʼtosuaʼisuʼuile, ʼuʼyuuʼigʼsame aʼgdluʼuʼuʼtsʼs

When my grandfather, Abel Frederiksen was alive, he used to tell a story about a hunting trip near Simiutaruaq. He came across three polar bears who had just killed a seal. When they saw my grandfather, they ran away and every so often one of them stood up on his hind legs like a hare to see if they were being pursued. My grandfather said he had never seen anything so magnificent. He brought home the dead seal they had left behind.

I have never been lucky enough to see a polar bear, but once when I was out hunting one on the ice along the Western shore, we came across the tracks of a bear.

tássa áma takoïdlóïdlugo simiutarssúp sujatáne upenagssá-
tut átagigaluara Abil Frederiksen avangmut kajartordlu-
ne nanorssuit pingajoïxat takusimavai, ugssuk nanoïtax
pissarigát takutdletioïmatik tapikángalermalāma tāmā-
simaufitik nāsimariarmassuk pisarssuat tiguïnarsima-
va, avangmut kimúmata takoranermerarsimavai pingajoï-
ssuángöx ukatdliïut nikuïvdlune assamut narajortalerá-
game piniagagssarssuit pilerïnarsimassusé   taimani-
me áma kajaïnarmik angatdlatexarïaratdlaramik pisagssa-
lik nūmagilertaratdlaïmatigït.

        uvanga sule nānumik takusimángïlangatamä
marssue takusimavaka avangmut angatártalerxaranïa
atátakut ïlagalugít.

                              Thomas Frederiksen

About thirty years ago, my father bought a motorboat. It was twenty-two feet long and cost only $180. When I first started to fish, we used to go out to the coast near Saattut and fish alongside the fishermen from the Roe Islands. When they fished close to the banks there, they could fill their boats with cod in no time at all.

Those were the times when cod was plentiful. When they finished, their boats were always full. We caught plenty, too, because fishing from a motorboat is a lot easier than from a rowboat.

In the winter, when the fishing season was over, the motor- boat gave us a lot more fun, because it was perfect for hunting walruses, seals and white whales. All the time I was a boy, I listened to all the tales about hunting trips and longed for the day when I would be old enough to go along.

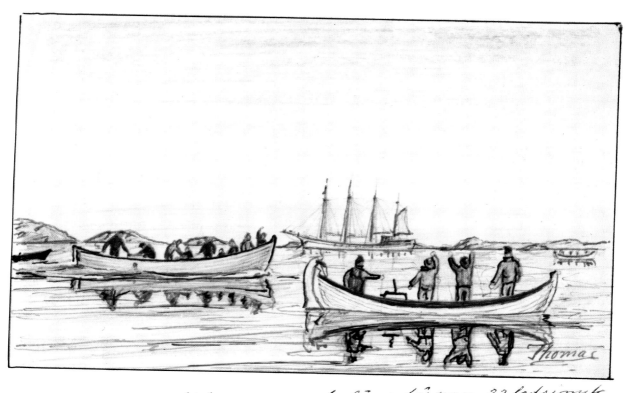

1946 me atâtango pujortulisartârpor 22 febsimule
1.200 kr. akuxarunarpor taimane misârdlunga ava-
tivtínut Sûtsunut aulisariartarpungut, ilârxâr-
dlunga Savalingmiormiut kisarsimârtut umia-
tsiartât aulisaxatigisarqravut ilâne avunga i-
kardlumut aulisariarâgamik kajagdlânardlu-
tik uterarant uligtânigdllutik.
               taimanme sârugdllaxaxor, sôru-
name umiarssuartik uligtânigdllugo avalâ-
put, âma atâtagkut sâr ugdligtaxaut, pujor-
tulixalerdlunume umiatsiânarnik pisauxue-
xuxor âma ulingtut îluatentigexârqut aor-
fît eqsunt xilalugtaxolls pisarisarpait îla ti-
kikeâgamik oxalugtuât niaxertaxaut xuxorna-
kalutigdllo îlâsalixnigaxax eiximax. kîleixume
utfît xagxemaxaxsimaxut tâama.
ne angumeritixsrnmaxut, mâma. Thomas Frederiksen
li nânukisavntele auexpaxrusnanartarpox nulisdllugt

Later on, my father bought another motorboat. It was twenty-two feet long also, but it had a tarpaulin cover over it, which made it better for fishing out in the open sea. The price of boats keeps rising. This new boat cost $1,550.

And it was in this boat that my older brother and I were taught how to sail and fish. Before I started, my brother used to go out and fish with long lines with my father near Saattut. Even in rough weather they would come home with the boat filled to the gunwhales with gutted cod, which they would trade.

áma atátanga pujorttulèrartàrigpok avatasiu-
tasingnàssumik rinungmat 22 fods lik kalilikpi-
lingnerarpok ilane avatáne anorisiutigisarar-
put ajúngenaok orpaxigkaluarpax 11,000 krúme-
karpok agatdllatit akitsoralugtuinaramik.

      lássalo perorssátigisarput imarsiutiku-
minartúngúgame kalerleriatunerilorfágdlússa-
kaok, katángutigingrínàudluta Pitalo angatdla-
Iigisarparpuk sujugdlermik mérágatdlara-
ma angajora atátangalo nigigtagkerssorlarput
avatáne áma sàtune pujorttulérratalo aigpá a-
lotdluarparput taunalo anordleraluartumilúnit
sárugdlingmik lisarigkamik iligkárdluge lunini-
assutigalugo iluararor

                  Thomas Frederiksen
                     Jgm.

I was still quite young when I started fishing with long lines in the open sea with my older brother Peter. I remember very vividly the first time we got caught by a southwesterly storm. There were just the two of us and a boy of my age from Attu. At one point, with the wind behind us, we were hit by an enormous wave and nearly capsized. And when we finally managed to get round to the lee side of an island, the boat was half full of water because the tarpaulin cover had been blown off the hatch.

Thomas Frederiksen

inusugtuarángoráma Pítalo avatáne nigigtag
kerssortarpungut, amalo puyortulîsarput kaleka-
biúrssox Augserniap avatâne kciángassuarmut
pukasarditelluta, anorioronicamera iláodluga taimane Agtorniumik inusugtuarcamik ilutiorvik
iláserorarpungut. — sujugdlermík orcunsigtealuar-
dluta scardiqdluta sangnikātördluta kásaleriôor-
dluta (kíngunga japapugdlluta) sangniktnararavta
assummkacuck igerdlavdlluta tússukaravta, orcu-
zpungut onasakcangut Hástíta matua katacteá-
tigo tônagsimaskaluta nátagutollo katagardlugit
nikunakaox atorcáxdlugo "mísísitutelle niuóns tu.k.

7 March 1957

This winter has been unusually mild with good catches of fish. The cold and dark is still noticeable on the return trips home. But with the spring coming, the sun rides high over the western icepack, where many animals are on the move. It is more and more tempting, and as usual, whether it is day or night, we head for there in our beloved motorboat. We are young, eager, always ready to hunt, full of fun and always kidding about.

Our best shot, my 21-year-old brother Peter, steers the boat. I am 17 years old and in charge of the motor. And as a result, I am always dirty. My younger brother Lars, who has just turned 15 and has just started to sail and hunt, is with us as well as another boy almost my age. We have lots of fun, especially the two younger ones. Now and then, they start wrestling. They remind me a little of two big puppies, always testing their strength.

As I write in my journal, it is getting on towards evening. It is twelve hours since we left home, and we are getting near the western icepack.

1957-me
    ukiok puvdluarmartok isse kaperdlagdlo kangiukiat-
tulerssok pissarigssuardlaarsimaodluta, avatane sikorssuit piniagagssakakissut kajugernarsikutortut, sekinekki-
agtalusimiline Mars, uleturmime unuaru-ilai'o ilerrutitu-
nasit pujortulérânguavtinik avang mukârpungut lii.mo
ta kimakaugut inusugtuinâvugu'me pileritorugtorneritakor-
na'tinilo kulanatlagssak ajornângekaok. - angaj ugdlerssarput
Pita 21-nik ukiulik autdlânagdlaskigssok(akugtok) nalungati-
gavtigo uvangalo akugtuvdlungalo mistaliagama pajaarsarpu-
nga itnik ukiokardlunga nukatalo Larse 15-ninik ukiulik a-
persset timat ilagisulerpatput ilausorputdlo Jørgen Rasmusen
ilutiga. ássul sangmisarput tâuna Agtormiussok, unag-
ssârniatdlutik ilane upanagsâput patigtâniatdlutik,
ilame kuianartakat sordlo nutarkat mukaungmiulut.
    lassa uvdlotsiutivne 7 Marts 1957. agdlagsimassok erka-
massata maligdlugo unulerssok sikorssuit naniqdliter-
dlugit 12 timi igetdlarerdluta.

                    Thomas Frederiksen.
                        Jgn

8 March 1957

Today we shot a fierce walrus and its one year old calf. It is difficult to get near walruses on ice floes with a motorboat, so we always bring a kayak with us. That works well and does not scare the game away. The walrus we shot was almost fully grown and filled the hold of the boat, so we sailed on and reached the open water, about 24 hours from the coast. Our plan is to get to Attu, a small village where we can sell our catch.

9 March 1957

We reached the western icepack. There we sighted white whale and began to hunt it in a rising gale. We caught the whale just before dusk, towed it to the leeside of a small iceberg and hove up there overnight because it was impossible to reach the coast against the north wind.

8 Mât#: 1937. igdlâlik nuarusartôk auuna pisaruerput naumsan-
taraua: iluannuvigisavârput sikuit akavniutáuk sláre Aatkaudài-
mik pulaterpigalugit auuásarmiata kaluét nángimenung-
mat. âma imánarme sengter pisarérsardtigd pisilelaku-
gut tingmukasdlutalé sikuit akaumsigut igerdlasdlula â-
ma imáutâ tinuit ivallormuk igerdlasariâvex, sikuulé
sigmarneik pulatlaugisaspavut. Agfumnutdlé tuniun
âvungut.

9. Mais sikorssuit kitdlligat tikiparput kilalagarssuan toku-
leráitge anordliteraluartôk maleraserdlugo pisarârput tais:
ork kåligdluge iluliángúp okuane únunvungut avungasig-
ssuax timukatpuungimat.

10 March 1957

When the terrifying stormy night was over and dawn came, we saw that huge ice floes had been broken into small pieces. We did find an ice floe large enough to haul the white whale on to and flenshed its hide off. We left the meat behind it had gone bad from being in the water too long. My older brother knew the way to our destination very well, so we had already begun to estimate what time we would arrive as we stood on the ice cutting the blubber from the whale's hide.

As we sailed on between the ice flows we caught two more walruses, and now the motorboat was full to overflowing. But we were now getting closer to the coast. The weather started to change, however, with a cold air from the north replacing the calm.

10 Maris 1957

umiaĸ amilânnartoĸ kâgʼrupeʁsunauvfa tugdligssâ ajornen uv-
dlânĸorpeĸ atorsatordlunilo kisiangne sikut seĸumissimaĸaut-
palatlïordluta pútaĸ amasiatʼĸisinausseĸ tikikavtigo pilaʁ-
fiĸârput pajortulêrkevtinipeĸ Erneʁ, J. Rasmusen. uvanga. Pʼátan.
kartaralo pútamïpungut. mátâ orssualonꝛꝛꝛloꝛuligkârutigꝛaut
âmâ neĸa utorĸasimanermik kajortʼisimagame lamât tigú-
ngilarput âmame suꝛꝛꝛmik kaligkaʼtigo puꝛꝛꝛkaʼtʼisimagame,
         uligkâravla kivigajagdluta limakarpagut 10 Mars
âma siko sinerdlugo aorʼtit mardluk pisariga'tigit nuá-
neĸavr mátʼsuganerssuaĸ imisâraluardlune nuna ĸa-
nigdligʼpuldlo kâtsivdlune avânĸasigâsiʼt suersiartoʼtpeĸ
orĸꝛꝛꝛtuĸsɔgautale ajúngilaĸ angajugdlersatʼale arĸu-
to nalánĸekringmago mátâʼt orssuialerpagut tikiutʼisar-
put erĸornarêrdlugo.

         Thomas Frederiksen
              Iginiarfik.

11 March 1957

It is before daybreak on the morning of King Frederik IX's birthday. While my older brother was steering the boat, all of a sudden there was a crash. We had hit a reef. The boat started to keel steeply over, and we were all thrown to one side. Right away, we started to throw our load overboard. But the skin of the walrus on top got caught, jamming the opening of the hold and could not be moved. We were in shallow water and even with the motor going we could not get refloated. There would be a long wait for the tide. We took turns in standing watch. All of a sudden I noticed that water was getting in at the stern of the boat, and the pieces of whale blubber on the deck were being washed away. Since everything looked so hopeless, I suggested to my older brother that he should ferry us one at a time to the nearest island on the kayak. And if we could not balance on the deck of the kayak, he should tow us in the water. We knew we were now in real trouble and were very nervous. Nobody wanted to be first, so I volunteered. When we reached land, I was freezing cold from the icy water. And as I stood there on the little island and waited for the others, all of a sudden I felt terribly lonely.

11 Marts 1957

11 Marts kúnge Frederik IKiminvigsratsok uvdlugssakut 1957
pingasûvdluta Otsuiávungut angajugdleissarput akugtok târ si-
simaleretssok nunat akornanut pulâmakaula igerdlaniardlu-
ta lâssangainarssuak kângortordlo pisorpalugssuak kisimiuvok
misigilêtpungut igdluinânut piorardlutâ ikardlipungut uve-
rujugssuardluta, - etkâniataluarpungut aotfitdle amerssuak nag-
dliugamik uvertugutdlo tâtokiûssimagamik ajornakaut. nal 20
kardlipungut tinimôrpok liningakaordle maskinamik kângat nutalu-
arétavta unitinarparpul initâne isersimârpungut akaantto sisuartor-
dluta kagdlutingísâmat kujanakaordle anore inotiarkormat. nal 18
ulimûlerpok anotsatigsiartorkilerpok akua alagkarialdlatiga ô-
sut sâvigaletsimasul akua agpardlume kagdlûsimavok kiviar-
ulerdlutalo nal 24 ilagka okarfigâka "okua imatssuarmik uligkâi-
simavok "Pilap akivânga "kalokiuh" akivara, kiviartulerpungut kagdlûi-
magâla, nagdlartitinartok okarfigâra "ikungo kererlârtom! ikâsotnia+
igut kairamik usiarsinângikutigut kaligléssuatigut, kâu rap kilerutépe-
darpra kangale pétérpui agdlamut sépunga kisatdlungalo ilagka iker-
uglatusimasut uvanga ikinakâga kâgalenigdlâydlak unerkigsardlug-
kertâtânguamat ikatererdlugalo aitsal kiseitdliumeraluarpunga manûiss

12 March 1957

Alone on that little island, I felt completely helpless. My legs felt heavy, and my clothes started to freeze. Thinking that maybe I woul[d] be the only one to be saved, I went on my knees and raised my clasped hands towards heaven in anxiety. When the others finally did reach the island, I was not only relieved but felt stronger. We were young and strong, and it was our duty to look after our parents and serve our country well.

My older brother gave us a pair of oars and some of the blubber to eat, and then set off towards Attu, without his parka because it had been lost in the sea. We remained on the island, wet, thirsty and sleepless. We started to run to keep warm. I could feel that the wind was rising. The others were getting nervous, and were beginning to feel drowsy. I knew it would be fatal to sleep in such cold, and so I did my utmost to keep them awake. My younger brother, the other boy and myself started to run and wrestle again to keep warm.

When the two boys seemed happier, I walked away from them and prayed to God that he would protect my brother who was trying to get help in the kayak. After that, I felt my strength come back. Soon it was possible to make out the half-sunken motorboat. And at daybreak we heard engine noise, which then faded away. A little later we saw a motorboat on the way from Aqisserniaq. It was "Margrethe" with the priest who was on service calls. A little later, it returned with another boat, "Karlsen." Our motorboat was raised and tied between the two larger boats. Before long, we were safe in Attu.

¹³/₃ 5⁷ nerent āranguamut pingame angn·ildi·timenge nihen;
nākaut masakigama a·isakalo kerrutiterd·lutik, iiānguagka a-
junāssagaluarpata etkāner saperavko kisima ānagtūnigssate, serku-
ngmetpuga" ünerssurudlugalo, ilalo erkigsiatdlekauga iiānguag-
kalamatmik ikārmata inūsagtūvuguīme angajorkagut nunar-
putdlo suligesūniagagssaralugit ánersākutdlo nunappissūneta-
la kānīpungut Guliudle aissaisa pissarssuit atānīgdlula·-!

Pilap magtangmik takugsserdluta nanetuarfötardlo ipu-
litidlo mardluk nīonatdlugit Agluliardlune kāinamik autdlatpok a-
norssarigsisotssāvok arkutigssalo sarfakalune akuerosakāngi-
tax nākāsunuli·lāvdlune sāvigsimangmat, uvagutdlo masakaluta
siningitötkartarsimardluta imetusokalutali kerertāranguar kāvig-
dlugö ūnagsārpugut saersigalugtuinarmat iiānguagkā etnumaler-
gut malugaka inatusogtutdlo ekersardlugit issekingmat iiingitō-
kinangmata okalugpavka ilausorputdlo nikatdliorkajānetsāvok a-
ngajugdletsāta kajānigsānik okalugdlune iniliormatkuinaknu-
kartāralo arpaliugtaletātine unalerdlune okarpok "nukarigssamāssit"
okatsigāka "āitsāt patigtāuf·isāngotpor patigtāniatitik" patitātukosīngoti-
aramik kisa igdlattalerput. kimaleriatmate tatriatdlariatdluga kajar-
tarput "ajungakāngitsamut sernigerkuare iiānguagkalo tikikaleit nuānā-
kauga sördlume akuetinekartunge. avatiotine pujottulērak kives
kasok etsilārdlunilūna nukartātalo lārse okarpok "sördlo sing nagtuku
lörssuam. kisa kāunarsimaletsoк lukutötpalugsialerpungut laimāgdlo
nipāruvdlune kijotna Akigsetniaptunjānik erserpor sunāvfā Nargrethe,
Palase agatdlagdluge Agtu milek nāmagtörsimagā Akigsetniamutdle ikitligsāsor-
simasut Karlsen,ip Margrithiodle akornāne pujottulērak imātparput Agtumut·iluumik p
nukagātpungu¡

April 1957

Since our accident in March, we continued our hunting expeditions with great success. On April 10th, after we had been to the Bay of Disko, we sailed out from the coast out towards the western icepack. But when the northern wind got stronger, we turned around and made harbour in Attu. We knew that several boats were still out: "Margarethe," "Karlsen," "Ujarlilooq" ("Forever Searching") and "Angerlartorsuaq" ("the one named after a deceased"). On April 11th the north wind was still rising, approaching hurricane force. On April 13th we heard the crew of the "Karlsen" on the radio, reporting they had reached Itilleq, south of Holsteinborg. We immediately asked if the other boats from Aqisserniaq had reached port, but were told there was still no sign of them. By April 14th, "Margarethe" had still not arrived home at Iginniarfik (the bird hunting area). But shortly afterwards, we heard that "Margarethe" and "Ujarlilooq" had reached Itilleq. "Angerlartorsuaq" had sunk, but the crew had been saved by the "Margarethe". Another boat, the "Elsinore" had been forced aground on Sukkertoppen (The Sugar Top) and two other boats from Itilleq and Sarfannguaq had disappeared with their crews.

This drawing shows "Margarethe," with "Ujarlilooq" nearby, picking up the crew from "Angerlartorsuaq" which is only a 20 foot boat and very old. The rescue took place shortly before the hurricane arrived.

34

1957 upernagssagkut umiugajangnita kigssina pisakameudluarpa-
ngut angalâttuardllutalo Diskobugtinut agdlât angalaxerdluta 16 Abril
avangnukatalu at alute avangnar/sanangnex suersiat tuinarmat
Agtumut pinararta numarkatigut Margrethe, kut Axrgsernuarmiut-
dle "Karlsen,, "Ujardliter,, "Angerdlartorssuardle,, avangmukarsimáput
Agtumitungut 11 Abril avangnex suerpox âma akagúkut anorer-
ssuartorssuver 13-a "Karlsen,, Itrdlimut nùnisimardlane numar-
katilik tikisimanasualugit radiúkut tusarmarpat Axrgsernumut
tusarniévungut tikisimángitdlatdle âma 14 Abil Iginierfingmut
âma "Margrethe,, pilarutingitsexsimaver tauvale radiúkut tuselerpe-
ngut Itrdlimut nùnisimassut "Margrethe,, "Ujardliter,, dle "Angerdlar-
torssuak,, kivisimaver inuile "Margrithemut tkisimáput tamarmig-
dle ajesalik "Elsenúta, Hanitsumut nùnisimaver kevunga Itrdli-
mialdle seitánguarmiutdle ajanarsimáput pujer tulerkat marta

kulóne titertungara tassa Margrithip Angerdlartor-
ssuak, pilugsimardlugo isukartarnarsingmat sujaalapiluta
nusugdluge kiviartulermat rnue itkimiterúk, imakamariu-
átinarpât angaldlatinguax pisaivax 20 Pedsilik Timukarner-
mine atanaviángitaluarmat anererssuarme 12 nik nukûgssa-
siling me anáusinierner âma riugerssunissakingame inaisea-
náunigsaul pingarnerungame kujanawax nalivtinoajanárte
kángitealdlatame, táukule anoretssuatmile ajugautiginexat-
tut netsetnavissat kingulinguemisingxngnexatiginexeut tássáu-
pume uvavtitut pilersagagdlit sujunigssamilenerxilewextut ajer-
nawaerdle angaldlat angissxssugaluattex rnarexip aslunguta,
"sulile pissaunewarper,, tamakume atortitáxul pivdluarner-
mut avrkatigssatulx̄a. Thomas Frederiksen
Lätdlit âca navianartorristuuk isuginaségyildlat rkeú-
kunialúxut inunertik sujuliotitut dleatrsarxr

4 May 1957

We enjoyed wonderful weather in Diskobugten, the Bay of Disko, while we were hunting a shoal of white whales. The government health department boat "Bjarnov" and another boat from Nivaaq came along for company. Doctor Olsen was on his way to Angissat to treat a patient on the summer hunting ground, and took part in the whale hunt. But his shots were far too low to hit the whales.

We shot two when the whales came up right in front of our boat. After harpooning, we killed the largest of the two. Olerujuk (Big Ole) from Nivaaq in the third boat killed the other one we had shot. With the help from one of the sailors from the health department boat, we flayed our catch on an ice floe. After that we shared the meat of the two whales between the three boats.

The summer in Diskobugten can be beautiful, but now and then there will be some fierce storms in the fall, when there is a risk of being iced over. Great care is necessary, and it is important to know all the emergency harbours.

4 Maj 1957. Diskobugtime alianaik kitalungarpeussuit nâmâ-
têtravligit maletssulerssungut "Bjarnew" Nivârmiut ardlata-
rugit tikiúput sunâufa Agissamitsut nôparsimasotlakar-
mata nakotsep Olsen-ip takusarsimagai lâssamiâssitâ-
ma serkoralausatpok inersaruinatome.

       tarmane sujuninguatotâtigut mardluk aut-
dlâgavligit pisarâvut angissok kalusingtâtigo nâle-
rêtdlugo Olsen ujugkut Nivârmiut isertak artulersi-
tarput kamavdlugo nagikaut pilagpungut "Bjarnew"
p kivfasailât tkiotsiavdlugo ilagut tikiungmata augu-
arpagut kilalugkat mardluk angatdlatit pingasivdlu-
ta nuânekaok mânalo sila alianaik zussame âmu
alianâgtaxaok aulisagaxakalumilo. Diskobugt ilâmle i-
mânâmpivigssumik anot. Thomas Frederiksen
dlirtarpox sualungmile u-
kiakut sianisârnastakaok   Igm.
umiatsialinitdle nalunagit kimâriarfigalugit
ajunpnerusaraluarput nalnârdlumik uersaka
jârnartarpox sualungmile nunat agssuane
silut exiteritut orusglauninartângikalua-
kait, — nenterdlutik : qusurnisaromile

The winter of 1958 was very good for the seal hunt. At times we would have up to 18 seals in our house. We three brothers caught seals in Alanngorsuak, a fjord that never froze because of a strong current. Every day we drove 5 miles in a dogsleigh to get there. My father, Jorgen Frederiksen, caught a lot of seals by net; in three months we caught about 200. My mother Regina, who was the district midwife, was untiring in looking after our catch. Only our sister was too young to help. Our young brother and three of his friends helped, and also went out hunting when they had a day off from school. Everybody in the district caught plenty of seals.

As long as the ice pack is close to Attu and Kangaatsiaq there is always good hunting in the district.

Thomas F.

1958 ukiok pitsak sikorenaok puisenavalunile uvdlut
ilâne puisit 18 igdluutinut kiteiitarpavut uvangut ka-
taingutigik pingasuvdluta Alángorssuarmut anguni-
artarpungut kilerdlitut umiatsialisimasarpungut I-
gimiarfingmuk km 8 simugsertarpungut nuáner-
taraok äuna atâtanga Jörgen Frederiksen napituaraok
uvdlormut ilâne 8 kiteiitarpai kaumatine pingasu-
ne 200 erkâne puisitaravut anânarput nersumakaok
Júnaijusor Igimiarfingme Regine Frederiksen anguta-
narssússugut ikiortuarpätigut amartaduarput
mirâgame nukagpiarkatelle pingassut ilnakusâri-
sartarput ilânusugtavalutigelle alnángiorfingmi-
ne nunarkatigut äuna pisakardluartarput erkâ-
mingutelle. Agto Kanjâtsiardlo puisartaraut sualungmile avatâi sikortulâmatararmik

October 1958

We sometimes go into Nassuttooq, the north part of Stromfjord, to trap fox. On October 30th I trapped a white fox and a blue fox. It is always great to hunt. In November, when we arrived home from the hunt we had caught 1 seal, 13 foxes, 2 hares, 1 skaru, 63 eiderbirds, and 7 puffins. On most hunting trips there are usually some hardships, but we tend to recall the good times the most. In the spring, as long as the ice is safe, we can use the dogsleigh to check our fox traps. During a summer with little bad weather, you always catch many more foxes. Fox hunting is always exciting, but can also be exhausting, especially if there is a lot of snow.

OKTOBER 1958 Nagsugtúmut teriangniarniaravta puldlaser-
soriartordluta tássane kakortak kernerdlo pisaráka 30
Okt. nuánekaok angalârdlune Novemberimilo tikípungut
pisarisimavdlugit natsigdlak 1 teriangnigssat 13 ukatdlitz
okaitsok 1 merkit 63 agpat 7, áma pissanganat tokattat-
pok angalanerup nagsatarisertagânik nuánekutâsunig-
dlo erdlavilârtardlunime nuánetsson kaningnerusarpok
upernagssábut ker mugsinile puldlasiartarput siko aug-
dlune atugagssâjúmârtínago, au. Thomas Frederiksen
esáleut silardlúlilajuppatdlânipikaugat   Igni.
teriangmannnenisarpok. nuánekawaok iláne aputekarpat
dláságme seawnahnjortaralungpok.

17 February 1959

The Strait of Alanngorsuaq is slow to freeze over because of a strong current. At last, it has frozen. Every winter we ferry travellers by sleigh to Niaqornaarsuk a village on the other side. This year we took two policemen, an Eskimo and a Dane, over the frozen strait without a boat. Because it was very cold, they did not have their uniforms on.

To freight people, dogs and equipment by boat in extreme cold can be very dangerous, and calls for great skill and care. It can be extremely hazardous when boats ice over, especially at night. Think that in the old days hide-covered women's boats were used for freighting. Sometimes we sailed in freezing fog and could not see a thing, and the only way to navigate was to sail by the direction of the wind.

In large open areas in the ice large flocks of seabirds congregate. All the birds we used to catch there were a good supplement to our winter food stocks. When I see those seabirds in these openings in the ice, I always think of a legend about the great hunter Qattaaq, who went out to catch eiderbirds far from the coast.

17 Februar, 1938. Alángorssuak ukiut 35 sikusimanane si-
kuδlarmat. alertilingmik ángalártunik ikássuilórtordluta kisame Niakornárssungmik kimugsit nangminek ikárput tássa Politit kalâlek kavdlunárdlo Ukalilik alángorkuvdlugo Tasi-
ussârssûp tungánut ingerdlârtut. Polititut Undiformekaratik ilisimangmat
Taimâtuánartássagaluaramik ikássurnek imarlúngika-
luarlok ilâne sinisârnarlakigame pujoragssuak ilâne ser-
mernarlakigame sikualuitdlo anerdlersume târsitivdlugo
aperkajánarlakigamik sikunialitdlarmat sulerikássurnek ar-
torsornarnerulerame ilame sermernek isse ajutôraluarûtalo
avangut akisugsârtigalugôt ikâtagut âle sujugdlermik umiamik
ikâssuisorsimasut. ilikardlugule ajungilak pujoragssuarme ava-
lagkâgauta okumigdluta apûtilissangut âssordlutasaunap tugâmik
anorssârtuartarame issilerútorâgat nunanile ersitsorâingi-
kaluartok nalunarnek Thomas Fredriksen
ájorpok. sumukagssavdlume.

Ign.

sikokingmat merkit angmalagtisut pisârutigâvut imar-
nersatuánguit tingmiarugssat imarmiut najorniartaking-
matigit erkârkajánerpok "Kâtâkut miterniarnerat"

It is said that Qattaaq always was an eager hunter, even when he was old. Once when the sea was frozen over, he climbed to the top of a nearby hill to look out for the possibility of a catch. Far out on the ice he noticed frost fog rising from a couple of places.

Early the next morning he took off with his two sons and a stepson. Far out from the shore they discovered a hole in the ice where there were plenty of eiderbirds. After a while they realized that they had caught so many that they would have to stop. But on the way back to the coast they noticed that the ice floes they were crossing had started to drift out. Obviously a storm was brewing.

44

Kátârâk utorkakasi uvdlune pileritorâok ilânigôr sikutdlat-
mat karkat portunersiariardlugit nasigkame tasamaner-
ssuar pajotáîat ûgaterisugartutlakuai.

âtetame avangmut rugukut erinine mardlute einersianilerio
galugit sagdlerânguit kapisimalerdlugit imatnereautikipât
miterpassuit ruánersiseritotât utorkertât pikerpok "nagsaterssuse keui-
arsigit, tauvamiuko nangmássatik sisnilivdlardlugit. tunungmukar-
niardlutik nunasarnetssuarmik sèvitâpat.

They were driven out to sea and eventually landed at Akilineq on the coast of Canada. There the stepson was killed by a stranger during an armwrestling contest. Qattaaq challenged the murderer, defeated him, and then killed him. Later they found out that the stranger always killed his guests.

Qattaaq always wore a lemming as an amulet. The lemming saved their lives and even brought the stepson back to life. After that, they met a witch, who tried to bewitch them so they would die. But when Qattaaq and his sons also wore pieces of bearskin as amulets, these enabled them to jump into the sea and take on the form of three polarbears.

When the stepson, who wore a snowsparrow as an amulet, was afraid of being left behind, the bears shouted "Why don't you use your small wings or else the witch Apiakasik will take you." And all of a sudden he was transformed into a snowsparrow. So they were all able to get back over the sea and reached home safely.

uisagamik sauitaput akilinermutdlo pingamik er-
nersiata Akilinermiorssuak pakasungmika igsuertipor-
dle angutrsialo sagsarame tanarssuakasik tokúpâ. sunauvfa tekerartiminik úmatitsisarsimángitsoe úumangmisartorssuak.

ernetsiane úmarteséramiuk avingátime ánámautik kima-
put Apiakasik putusukasingormat nanoraminatsianigdloátnu-
akatamik nanúngordlutik imánut terkáput ernersiale ku-
palotatsúnguamik arnualik nagalermat avatáne nanorssu-
ít terdlulákaut. Apiakasip netinássakautit sisoriatdlutit isat-
kilagaluakil, kupeloserossingormat ikárput.

9 March 1959

Outside our hamlet, where I go ice fishing, I caught 23 flounders, 2 isinger, 1 crab and 1 skolast. Small flounders are useful for feeding the dogs. But since they are very tasty, we often eat them as a change from our daily diet of seal meat. Travellers passing through our hamlet also buy food for their dogs. For a short while the Royal Greenland Trading Company tried trading flounders but they soon gave that up when they realized that trading in seal meat paid a lot better for the hunters. Methods of hunting and fishing are always being changed and improved to suit local conditions. At our hamlet we have been using "gliders" to lay down our long fishing lines under the ice. A hole is made in the ice, and a square metal plate with extra weights on it is dropped into the water. The "glider" drifts through the water and reaches the bottom far away from the hole, so the rest of the fishing line with the hooks on it is drawn gradually after it and in that way is stretched out over the floor of the sea without being tangled.

Thomas Fr

9 Marts 1959 ikiutine kaleralingniartunga taimane
23-nârpunga anûtat2 sâtuak'saviuvdlopûa, pisatôka.
    kaleralerkal kingminul nerisariti vdlugit iluakaut
âmame mamakigamik nekinut avdlánissutausaramik
angalasutdlume piumarait kingminul netukautigissa-
ramigkik. ilâme âkajâkasiussarput tunisâtsiaralaer-
put akikitsûvdlutigele. Handelimik misilingnerata-
luatame tg angunatkunekartul angúng-itsörpait
iluamik sangminekánginamik pursingniarner sang
minekarnerugame pingârtumik kagsuserssotnek
akigssatsinarnetungmat.

            Thomas Frederiksen
                    Tgn.

sûtdlûnit pimarname auliarnermule nagsâju-
ssut aikusartume, sikunee ajortumule iluanutâsa-
lo iluarsiautortardlutit. uvant sârdlisitoe ator-
nenarpet ~~sikms~~   sike putoriardluge ~~rigdlidioramima~~ o-
~~eimâlutatoielege~~ migimuartarput ~~-~~ sârdlisâtou
~~tigppat~~ aninygatikuardluge, kisatâ ditit it ~~unuimijue~~ -

1 May 1959

Here we are seen hunting white whales in the Bay of Disko
north of Ikamiut beyond Upernavik. While we were on shore
on lookout, a hunter by the name of Johan from Ikamiut
came by on his dogsleigh. It was a beautiful day with a warm
spring sun. We sat down and cooked seal meat over a fire
while he entertained us with exciting tales. However, since we
were in an area where there always were lots of white whales,
we continued to keep watch over the sea. By May 3rd we
were able to take home to Iginniarfik the remains of 22
white whales. We had an abundance of wonderful tasty
blubber.

Towards the east the Tussaaq Island is visible. Over to the
left behind the icebergs is Qasigianguit (Christianhaab),
where there are several shrimp beds, and also plenty of big
tasty sea cats. Lots of cod can be caught near the icebergs.
But you have to fish with great caution near the icebergs,
because they are inclined to keel over very suddenly.

1 Maj 1959 Diskobugdeme kilalungarmerdluta Ikamiut a-
vangnâne Upernavingme alianaekisor nasigdluta Ikami-
Ormior suât tikiungmat kimugsimik okaluasâtlor tusat-
nâsutigalugo nekitûpungut rgavdluta kiniutigalugo kila-
lugarale kinangmat ila alianaik sekisnek kialetssuak mânalo issikivigik nuân. —

          3 Maj Iginiarfingmut angerdlarpungut kilalug-
kat alautikôrtat 22 pisakakatâutigalugit mâtangung nange-
kaok.

          Thomas Frederiksen Iginiartok.

kagiutine Kasigiânguit nunâ iluliar —   Dr Egm.
ssuit nalâne assilissap talerpiatugâne kukurtak
Tupssâk ersipor. tamâna kagia kajakasfucarpok
Upernivirp kalôrfia anurdlakissumik, âna kera-
karfigpavossuakarstok innuka nalunguait mik-
teulo nerpigik. iluliarssuitallo krkait câng-
dlit nuânarinakait ulokianalâgmartaramik au-
lisarfigalugit aururiatâusínâsaramik.

7 May 1959

A long way from the shore, we came upon a herd of walruses. After killing six, we had no more room in the boat, so we sailed home. And on the way back we passed a big shoal of white whales. With a motorboat as small as ours, we can only do so much hunting.

As we neared the coast we were surprised by a northern storm. But we reached Attu safely. Sailing through a storm, everyone has certain duties that have to be performed, no matter how tired one is. Sailing past icebergs demands special care. If they are aground, or if they are beginning to break up, one should always sail by on the leeward side, since the water on the windward side is usually rough and can be full of small icebergs that are very dangerous for a boat.

7 Maj 1959. avatâne auverpavssuit ĭkĭpangut arfĭnierâr-
pungut uligkârsarsétuvdluta ĭmerarta tĭmukânanaugut
âma wĭlalangarpavssuit nâmătôraluarpavut ĭmarku-
kĭnĭpalâkasĭk-ấ,, igĭtaκângĭtaguidle

nunaκanigdligĭpuldle âma avúngasiup error?or mĭat-
sar,ĭlerpâtĭgut ĭmerartĭnanaox sarsar majorâsagor-
ssúgame apûtdluarpungutdle Bytamut. anorisuilursiv-
dlune ĭngĭssak suliar- Thoma Frederiksen
dle κĭmangnaôĭsârstari.
aκarput! κasugaluarǎvilúmĭt, Tya.
nĭk ĭpigdlugo, κârtigdlumĭlo nigdlâgdlagtĭgaine kĭâ-
κanga ĭlorfâgll! - âma aκugdlune maliarassuit
κârnerĭôrlumerĭt, agssorκungnĭartavauartarput!
sikutdlo aκornanigdllune ilulĭssat ĭkerdlĭsĭmavut
agssorκungnĭartaκaκanyĭtdlat! sarfavnigdllúmĭt. ⌐

29 May 1959

Once while I was in the Amerloq area south of Sisimuit, along with my younger brother Lars, we rescued a Dane. His motorboat had been grounded because of engine trouble and now was being driven towards the coast by a very strong wind. We towed him home to the hamlet Sarfannguaq, where he lived.

At that time the cod industry was declining. Only in very deep waters were cod still plentiful, and these we caught with long lines.

1 June 1959

At 9:30 p.m. on a beautiful evening we set out from Sisimiut along with Jens Geisler and his boat Aaveq (The Walrus). The next day at 3:00 p.m. we reached Iginniarfik to attend the confirmation of our only sister, Magdaline Frederiksen.

Aaveq was the first large fishing cutter with a harpoon canon for hunting whales. Jen and his brothers are pioneers in hunting from larger boats, and have inspired many other northern Eskimos to follow suit.

54

29 Maj 1959 κavane Amerdlu migdluta lârsdo κavdlunâ-pu-
jortulérât κamik únigtôrsimavdlune tipulâlerssoκ Sartanguí-
at, âpatpule Sunawfa Sisimiormio κavdlunâu nunasiní-
κoκ. larmane sugotnatigotnik sârugdlekardluángineru-
voκ ajunângilangutdle nigigtagkerssotlarpungut.

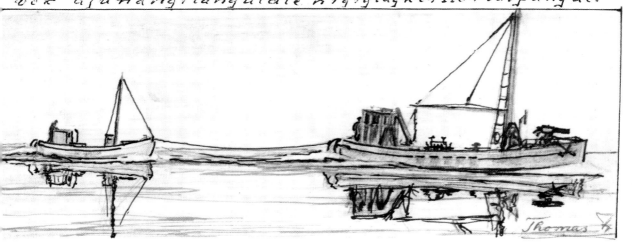

1 June 1959 imugkut nal 9½ Sisimiunik autdlarpungut Jens
Giesler-ip angatdlatâ "Rweu, igrakatigalago alianaik awangú-
kut nal. 13: Igminartingmut tikipungut arnartatuarputaper-
sestítoκ Magdalene Frederiksen. Rweu, pujortulirmat κamu-
tiligdlit sujagdleresarât' nunaotíne pumarnerudlo
tugatigut taκutitsisuvdluartuvoκ.' Jense κataruqutal
entúto aulariqtsut sulramúmutdlo brúmus merudlí-

1959

In the months of July and August there is still plenty of cod on the fishing banks, where we used to fish. A fully-loaded boat holds about 4,000 pounds of cod, which can be sold. Here we are shown at the "bank" fishing along-side "Jenskarl," "Skoburn," "Franz," "200" and "Margrethe."

Sometimes the sea can be completely calm like this. But cod are most plentiful when the current is the strongest and the sea is rough. Storskraapen, the seagulls, always appear where the shoals of cod are. It takes three hours to get out to the fishing banks, they are six miles from our hamlet.

When the cod season is over, we fish for seacats with long lines at Saattut until October. And a long way offshore are the flounder banks where there is always an abundance of fish. Towards the end of autumn when we start hunting seabirds around the fishing banks, we sometimes sail through large shoals of cod close to the surface, and sometimes large shoals of salmon.

1959. jul. Augustilo ovutistine skunen skardivotlo
sūragdlovartanaok. aulitsataxpungut uvangut 2 %oo
ericāne kītlasssarpungut.

   uvangut "Jens Karl" skooun, "Franz" Nozar, Margrethe.lo
skumer mr̄Pungut. anatā rlāne taimāitaraluarper mag-
dlerdlumilo sastfongdlumilo sārugdlovarneruserpeit punyar-
tumik ratsajusawa + Tivdlune

                     Thomas Fredriksen
                          Jgn.

sārugdlīt akutdlarungato Sātune rērarmartarpungut
Octobermut nyyglagarssortarpungut tamarmik J-
kardlordlo 6 milit myssānilgput 3 ime uvangut ormigtarpa-
vut nunavtinik. taijāna Store Kellersen Paula avatinut, au-
lisagawarfigssūrov rangale, rlāne agpangmiardlu-
ta uloilout skūnerssússonmardlugit agpaluyāstiv-
nerit sunāvfalulo sārugdlīt igerdlārtut ā-
ma taimangnagajalo kapisgdlīt igerdlaīt to-
kumewartarsimāgput rangerdllugssup kerfersioerfrup
pātuyāne piigsiqartonarlauārdlo uloilout.

12 December 1959

In the late fall, some blackside seals come into Alanngorsuaq Fjord. From November until February the seal hunt is always good, both from land and from motorboat. Here, I just have shot a formidable seal cow from land. On the other side of the hill my father is in hiding and has also shot one. The same day, my brothers shot several from the motorboat. Large herds of seal can often be seen in the Fjords. In the old days, we used to hunt from kayaks. Kayaks are still used, but mostly by the hunters from Niaqornaarsuk. We get a good price for the blubber and the pelts of the seals we catch. But nobody buys the meat, so it is shared amongst everybody at the hamlet.

12 December 1959, utiagkut atârssuit Alángortssuak puta-
sarpaut. Novemberimik ilâne Februarimut, pujortuленka-
mik nunamigdlo piniarnekartarput. - tássa Nûgssuarme
Tasiusârssup avangnâtungane, namavdlunge atâk igdlâlik pisariginga, táimane âma atâtanga kujatâtungi-
ne anguvor, igdlâlingmik âma ilagka pujortalerka-
mik angusimáput, imane ikera amisokartanaoir-
sujugdlermik kâunamik piniarnekartarput. sulime kâu-
nat atornekanaut pingârtumik Niakornârssungmiu-
nik. Alángorssuarme kapuinariajungnârsaluartut pi-
niagagssat sule! Thomas Frederiksen
natsersastanaore!

nunat nûgangtat kauigmavigssarpavsuanar-
put, agisunile agatdlaugmik imigsititeralumilo
julagtarfiútigisumile pujorartúput. sikorssuarne-
lumit ilunutârnanaoe! avatane

29 December 1959

At the Bay of Nuussuaq, during a grouse shoot, I shot 19 birds and ran out of bullets. There were many more grouse, but it was difficult to get near them because of the deep and soft snow.

When the weather is good, it is a joy to go grouse shooting. In the fall or the spring there are usually many grouse near the Fjord. Some people go grouse shooting with their dogsleighs and shoot a lot of game. But usually it is only the boys that shoot. But teachers and other employed people go grouse shooting, too, in their spare time.

29 Dec. 1959.

uvdlume Nûgssûp kangerdllumarnane avig-
serniarama 19 râdllungala nungûtigama avig-
suavaox aputdlo mâsararnavalune.

Thomas Frederiksen
Igimiasfik

avigsserpavõvsuit ulviâlvut upernagssâlvutdllo ka-
ngerdllungne igerdlâstarput. kimugaimigdlo piniar-
niarâne nâlârdlugit pivavarnartarsinavavox, aut-
dlainiardlumilo avângusivârfiussúngevavox sila-
yigtivetlugo kivisa piniartamiarâne agdlatitdle ä-
ma lumisâvdluavnuvlersinâuput, avlaguarvat a-
vigsserniarajuguerusaramit. apovitdlo atorpigdljtello si-
ngiôsfivguiane piniardlugit miâmarisavait.

February 1960

In Oqaatsut we catch seals with nets under the ice. Here I have just pulled up my catch through the ice. When the net is straightened out, it will be let go down under the ice again. In north Greenland that is the method they use. But out on the open waters in the fjord we catch from the motorboat, using heavier sea nets with good results.

Oqaatsut Island lies on the other side of Tasiusarsuaq, the great inland lake. In the winter, when the fjord freezes, we usually move our motorboat to Qiterleq, in the middle, which never freezes because of the strong current.

62

Thomas Fr.

1960 Februar.

Oraitsune napitortarpungut imamile pu-
portuliskamik anguardluta tässa napitortara ig-
dluârdlugit kagssutit âmutigluk amuânardlu-
git siârtarput uyarai tuydluiärdlugit näkariänä-
ngortisinardlugit oraitsut Tasiussârssup akiani-
put ukiuikut umiatsialisimasarfiata sikugângat köder
dlermut nûtarpungut.   Thomas frederiksen

Avangnâne sikuikut kagssuserssornik atorne-
kartareaox. Sikumerdle ajortune "imarssiutit,, â-
ma pisauarnartarsimakait kagssuserfiwollis-
artune.   puisit igerdlârfiäne ikumsârka-ntikuit
kapisiligtuit ama puisit talersfuartarput

2 May 1960

Yesterday we started out from Attu. Along the ice pack west of the Uummannaq Island we caught 2 walruses, 2 ring seals, a newborn ring seal and several puffins.

At this time of the year the catch is abundant in our area. In spite of that, we are sailing south to catch cod. It was foggy when I went to bed. My brother Peter and our passenger, who was also the pilot, sailed the boat. When they later woke me to relieve them they were satisfied that we had made good progress. And when the fog disappeared, I recognized the coast. Palasip-qaqqaa (The Priest Mountain) and Nasaasaaq (The Bitch's hat). They were unmistakable. The wind was strong and our fuel reserves were running low, so I suggested we go into Sisimiut. The other two said together, "But we passed Sisimiut a long time ago." "Look here," I started to explain: "in there I can see Palasipqaqqaa, and back there you can see Nasaasaaq, and now we are passing Qassit Island, which is mentioned in the saga as the island where the great killer Qaassuk lived." Our pilot looked confused. Peter just said, "Why don't you go closer to the coast?" But because of the strong side wind the boat was now rocking heavily. Our dory was on top of the deck, and survived only because it was well tied down.

I can't stop thinking of sagas about the kayaks from Amerloq. In a bad storm, the hunters were forced to land on the island of Qassit, exactly where their great and most feared enemy Qaassuk lived.

igpagsar Agtumik aulдlarpungut. Umanap sivдrne sikorssuarne
aotpit matdluk pisarigavtigit natsitdlo 2 natsiakasigdlo 1 agpat-
páluitdlo.—

pinagagsalermatúnátúglertotasit avaterput kujatánut
aulisariunarangut sårugdtil erxamalerdlugit uvnuar putsilersok
inatama Péta ilausotpatdlo ilisimesottarisarput iluáge aruglat.-
pardlarkariarmala arulerpunga pilerternetarlat etsitetsi mang-
mat nuna ilisarnagdlut "palasip karka, Nasaussatdlo sordlo kisimik
takotkusul ingerdlaviat kujangmut torxarsimatxaluardlugulo su-
látpul mildlingmut äma anorsarckingmat apetäka sisimianut
núnininanarumavedlunga akivanga "Sisimiut kangale kangeretxarti-
git" (sunävfa únuar etsiumeriarmat nuna Sisimiut etxatilisima-
gät)? Namitsul kanigdlereta vligit, ingerdlanarumagaluarlut u-
patuartútilerpavka "ápána "Palasip karka, ungatäne nuilersok "Na-
saussack, auna avarkyilerpatput "Kagsil, tássa Kägssagssúp ig-
dloxatfa" ilisimasortarput akúnaglortox Píta oxarpok "atagu-
me timutsakaluarniaril" sangnikakavta ingmetartinatsigalu-
arpok umiaussáretdlo userput aulajager serdluagágame atápá
iláne kartitdluartetaluardluta userigavtame, sisimianut pigav-
ta imägdlatäma kuxuglagpungut "siniexagdlunimiuna ikiaxotnar-
tox, erkängitsúngila ale "xáinat Amerdlarmiut anoterssuar-
mik támardlutit "Kägssung, mut tekexäxnerat"

Thomas Frederiksen,

Qaassuk from Qassit

The two hunters in kayaks from Amerloq had been surprised by a terrible storm during a hunting expedition on the open sea. And because it also started to snow, they were unable to find the way to their hamlet. As they paddled, they felt the storm suddenly go still, and with panic they realized they were near the homestead of their terrifying enemy, Qaassuk. When they reached the shore, Qaassuk was already on his way towards them, so they gave up any thought of running away. Before Qaassuk got to say anything the oldest of the kayakmen shouted, "We are here against our own will." Qaassuk answered: "Even if you are here against your will, you had better come onshore." Even though they feared they would be killed, they stepped out of their kayaks. Qaassuk said, "Come on up to my hut." When he turned and started to walk towards the hut they followed him, since they were exhausted and needed to get into a warm hut. It was obvious that Qaassuk was angry since he had never forgotten that his son was nearly killed by his enemies.

Kâgsuk. Kássine.

Amerdlormiúngôk kêunat mardluk uļorkat inúsuglor-
dlo avatânut kajartordlutik nigermik anotetssuaļi-
ugsáput etsingit nitautak tikiuteniarmat nûniusîgsat-
lik etkeniatnek sapiletamiko igerdlaniardlutik orku-
itutut ikamik piletiarpât "Kâgssúp, etsigisatssuat mik
nunânut pisimátdlatdlutik inússualo arajutsivekata-
ne tápika igdlumesâne takorêratik atiitersordlo unig-
titinartukagsáput. timagiutdlatmat orkángslátsâne u-
torkânerup okartigâ "tikerât niángipatdlátdiuta tikerâ-
ļetsujungut. akeká "tikerârniángipatdlátdluse tikerâļetu-
juse niukasiydluse, tokutâsangaterdlutigdlo ajornaning-
mat niuinarput Kâgsúp okartigai "sila taimáitok anêtſi-
úngilat majuakasigîtse!, majualigdlusmat malîna-
kaut âmame Amerdlume pisatigsángewigamik kasug-
dlutigdlo kiagtumut isetnigsartik tilanârtilângitsú-
sângilát. Kâgsugdle kiningâsimagame et ne kavane to-
kutârkajarnikúmat.

Thomas Frederiksen

When they reached the warm hut, they took off their parkas and sat down on the plank beds. Qaassuk became hospitable. He went out and fetched a selection of choice food and they began to eat. There was a sense of wealth about the hut. The furs covering the plank beds were the finest polar bear fur, and the walls were covered with fine reindeer skin. The brightness of oil lamps spoke of a lavish use of whale oil.

Qaassuk began to tell one story after another. Suddenly a yell was heard above the howling of the wind. Qaassuk went outside at once, and when he came back shortly afterwards, he said that his oldest son had just arrived back from the hunt with a large narwhale.

Qaassuk continued to tell more stories. Suddenly, while the guests were engrossed by the storyteller, their attention was disrupted by someone shouting, "Well, unwelcome guests!" When they looked towards the entrance of the hut, they noticed a harpoon being drawn back. A moment later the son came in and said: "If you had been ordinary guests, I would have killed you before I came in!"

igdluanut iseramik nangame kisâgdlak tuili-
tile pêramikeit igitutdlo Kâgssup inorersârfigilerpai
anigame nerisagssarssuit erneimagit nerritilerput.
Amerdlume pissâlerijutdle tâuterule pissâlereingua-
kilik nânut amimik nâgdlek itsait tutut amimar-
ssue nangame piamiagdlungue nâgdlualinguarse ruo-
dlé ikumagamik kisâgdlak iserdlugit. tâimana oka-
luytuak agpîpâ. anorerssuan nyorssugpalorugtulis-
ssox êrtarpaloxaon Kâgssub anigame iserdlmilo oka-
pox ernerssuane tikeitox nernertarssuarmik tilalugas-
simardlune okaluytuane naginarpâ tikerâvisa oka-
luytuarten alaganiarungnânugtordlugo okatdlarmet
"tikerârniângigpatdlâsdlutingôn tikerârmik kan
targanut kiviariatdllaramik tauvauna nansorssuak
tenilerssox. tinguninguna ernerssua iserpox. ''asule
tikerâkasiutivdluse isertinanga tapingapakâvse!''
                                        Thomas Frederiksen

When the guests got ready to go home Qaassuk gave them many presents and then said, "Don't dare to come visiting here again, or you'll be sacrificing yourselves." When the people of Amerloq saw all the many fine presents, it became impossible to dissuade them from going to visit Qaassuk. But on their way to visit him they were surprised by a storm and were forced back. Many of the hunters from Amerloq were drowned in the storm.

A poor old man, who lost his son that day, decided to have revenge on Qaassuk. Nobody believed him and they all laughed. In spite of that, the poor old man got his revenge this way: He persuaded a lot of kayaks to sail openly towards Qaassuk's hamlet. In the meantime, he and another old hunter landed on Qaassuk's island from the opposite side. And when they had crept up to Qaassuk's hut from behind they could see that he was on his guard. He was walking very restlessly in and out, keeping an eye on the kayaks that were approaching. He had set a loon as a lookout on his roof. Every time Qaassuk went into the house, the two old men crawled nearer the house. When the ice loon started to make noise announcing the danger, they heard Qaassuk say: "I see them. They cannot surprise me." Finally the two old men got to the entrance of the hut. They were trembling with excitement. After standing for a while looking towards the kayaks, Qaassuk turned around, lifting his arm to go in to the hut. That is when the poor old man shot his arrow into the armpit of Qaassuk and killed him on the spot. As he fell towards the wall of the hut, the other old man shot an arrow into Qaassuk's back.

tikerôt angerdlalermata tunukulôrdlugit okatfigigaluarpai
"kigârnagôk tikerârtokatdlariaunane tikerârtokaralua-
tunigôk nungutânginagsáput, nunarkalait nâlángitdlu-
lik autdlaraldlatamik pisarsinatigdlo uterpait anoxer-
ssualugssâudlutigdlo kajaussorpagssuit Amerdlu-
mut likingitsôrput, — utorkánguit ilât etnerssuane
kajáumat akimálerrilâunarack piniarlutrilâta igdlâti-
ngâ "ha-ha-ha-takusiuk kâgsugssuarmut akirniartugssak"
utorkánguatdle riuatsilivok kajarpayssuit kâgsit
avatânik limukartivdlugit utorkaralikasingminik
âiperdlune kâssit tunuatigut kâgsuk pagdlituterpait âring-
me likilerrarpaut anigune rserune agdlamutdlo kiviagsa-
nane kajarpayssuit tangânut. utorkánguit muteramik rser-
lordlo arpatusutunik anisordlo pisáput. kâgssup tigdlug-
ssuane kardluligdlarmat tapilta okarpatdlarack "/arajuti-
simângrilâkali, anisordlo pava likikamike kangasajingu-
arsikasit avatimiuna kisiat, kisiane isilerdlune unine
agsârimimago utorkángup pisikamike kanga kâruag-
dlak rimaterotdlugo torkúpâ" (aug. Thomas Frederiksen
pakaiata nulumârigut rragenâ)

Qaassuk's son married a girl from Ikkamiut (near The Sugartop) and made his home there. The girl was the only girl amongst many brothers, who all appreciated their brother-in-law very much, because he wasn't afraid of bad weather.

One day he came back home in his kayak, towing two large blackside seals, despite a heavy wind. Later on that evening, he started to scold his wife, something he had never done before. One of the brothers began defending his sister. After a pause, the brother-in-law started again, which caused the rest of the brothers also to get involved in defending their sister. They started to fight with the brother-in-law, but he was too strong for them. At one point, someone pulled a knife and plunged it into his stomach, but he tumbled all the brothers over, made for the entrance and ran outside in the cold with only pants and boots on. They chased him along Kangerluarsuk towards Appamiut, but they could not catch him and he finally disappeared amongst the cliffs along the shore.

Kâgssungân ernerssua Ikamiune ningáussimale-
rujor anguterpait arnartatuât nuliartârisimaga-
miuk sakiatsiarpavssuisale asavatdlârpaut anorâi-
narmut sapisángitsorssûmut.

ilâmâsit anorsaunigâ tikerpor âtârssuit mar-
dluke kaligdlugit úmigumalarssox taima puntser
nuliaminnut âmatdlaqqatulerpox sakiatnâta sem-
galugo nájane orxalúpâ uvfa mpagersimalarssor ni-
ngaormata akisalenarmago ilai ilârsuvdlutik su-
nigsâlerput orxâtorssuângordlutigdllo kîra paggasi-
naraut ningaorssuartite katurdlugo artulerdlugu-
le uvfa kirimûtsor kaimâgdlune ilâta saringnik a-
kuângut kaperâ serxâkamigit katangmut pisex-
taox kimâgdlunile mâtângax Kangerdluarssuk
ruterordlugo auunga Aqnamunrut ilaisa malrasi-
raluaramílco karkarssuk akornânrut sujuârât.

6 May 1960

This morning at about 7:00 a.m. when we were being towed
by "Bistrup" past Appamiut, I saw the Fjeld Inngik (The
Point) with only its summit showing above the fog. It brought
to mind that poem by Jakob Kjaer: "When I go from north
beach Ikkamiut, the large Fjeld
    will appear rough and broken at the middle but
    unmistakably high."
                    (Poem by Jakob Kjaer)

After passing Ikkamiut, we arrived at Maniitysoq (The
Sugar Top) at 2:00 p.m.

6 Maj 1960

Th. Frederiksen

uvdlâ Kangâmiunik nal. 7 Bistrup..mut, kaligtivdluta Ag-
pamiut sârkuvdlagit Junúkordluta Ingih pûtsumik ku-
lálungâ ersigtok takuara.

        'dvanga likikuvkit Ikamiut
        karkarssuar nuilmârpok
        maniildlune inauvok kitersmigut
        kigikamilô malungnarpok. —

Ikamiut sârkuvdlagit nal. 14°° Manitsumut pivungut
                      (Ikamiut kangerdluinut
kangitine Kâgssûp ernerâta kimâvtia Kangeraluarssup
                                 nunâ →

12 June 1961

On June 10th we were in the Isortoq Fjord (The Dirty) catching spring smelt. Just as we had filled our motorboat, the "Elsinore" came by. And since our nets still were full of Ammassat, we also filled their motorboat, and then we went into Maniitsoq to trade.

"Elsinore" carrying 13,000 pounds at 1 cent per pound earned $130.00; our 22-foot motorboat carrying 8,688 pounds earned $86.88.

On June 12th, just after the "Elsinore" had been loaded, Svend came and handed our skipper, Thomas Lennert, a telegram from his wife Mette, who is my cousin, announcing the birth of their son on June 10th.

Right after that we followed Svend to check his nets, but they were empty, so we returned to Maniitsoq. I set off again in our motorboat, and along with the "Elsinore" we arrived in Sisimiut on June 15th at 7:00 a.m. The next day we bought $420 worth of nets.

° 12 June 1961 °

10 June Isortume angmagsangmardluta ungusig-
ssitigut uligkâsrmata pujortulisarput dlo uligkâr-
dlume "Elsenôrre„ tikiungmat ikavunga sivnigut-
dlo ikeriardlungit icalorkigsinardluta kimukâs-
pungut 6500 kg°io 650 kroude pujortulisrauta 4344 kg
434,40 kr .

:012 June° "Elsenôrre„ p lâstra uligkâginartok Sven-
ikut tikiugput nâlangatputdlo Sisimiormio atêra Thomas
Kennett. ernertârsimavdlutik nulia igdlûsara Helle
radiorsimavok 10 June °

kimut tusardlunilo Svinigkut igrakatigalu-
git fungârnê Pakeriardlugit susârsimengmata Ma-
ntsumut igerdlânarpungut "Elsenôre„ me acupunga.

unugsiuvâtêrauta uvdlâgssakut "Elsemêrrikut
dlo avangnamut nunararfît arkusâgdlagtârdlu-
git. Sisimiunut 15 june nal 7, apupungut avaqugtaut
bungarnisivungut. Thomas Frederiksen
3000 ,00 kr.
                Iginiartik.

June-July 1961

After our arrival home from the south, with the smelt harvest over, we started to fish with two lines and two rowboats at Saattut. Our small motorboat was anchored between the islands, and before long it was loaded up with cleaned cod. We took turns in tending the lines. The catch was mainly cod, seacat and flounder. Usually a rowboat was filled every trip.

The prices were: First grade cod 2½ cents per pound. Cod, scaled but not cleaned, 1½ cents a pound. Flounder 7½ cents a pound.

9 July 1961

Today we are on our way to Iginniarfik to sell our catch. Our hull is full with fresh caught cleaned cod and seacats. And on the deck, we have three blue side seals we also caught.

Since my parents were invited to attend the visit of the Royal couple and the Princesses, we took in the long lines, stopped fishing for a while, and went home.

kujatánik titsikavta angmagseréravta sátunut nigigtag-
kersorpangut umiaussat matdluk nigigtagkatdlo takisút
matdluk atosdlugit pujortutórarput sátutiketasánut ki-
sardlugo angmat textikánik imertarparput. pátdlatáu-
dluta nigigtagkerisarpangut auna amuatlunga sárugdlit
kétkat natárnatdlu akingtarput amuatnex atausek umi-
aussar uligkátlatparput. (sárugdl. prima ¹/₂₅ ler pr kg. kennutorteg-
dllt ¹/₂₅ ler pr kg. kétk. ¹/₃₃ ler pr kg. nat. ¹/₂₅ la.

9 juli 1961 sátutiardluta pingassunik agdlagtúararavta
urdlume tuniniávungut Iginiarfingmut tássa sátsu-
rik kangimukartugut. sárugdlit kérkatello las-
tidiníput nulait erdlaviagtat. aulisátámarsorni-
savktungánut uligkátta-   Thomas Frederiksen
jártuarpungut.
(kángikut nuluakángigssardlo titrinivlermata amu-
  siavunguts 13-juli. átatálast áimmiávata

13 July 1961

Qunaaq a famous hunter from Tununngasoq, a former Member of Parliament from Greenland and a good friend of Piitarsuaq (Peter Freuchen) is dead.

In his younger days he was an exceptional hunter. In Nassuttooq he killed lots of reindeers. Every spring he caught many basking seals on the ice with the help of a shooting shield. He had dogs that looked just like all the other sleigh dogs, but they were famous for their training and their obedience to his secret signals.

Once Kunuunnguaq (Knud Rasmussen) and Qunaaq were travelling with some others towards Sisimiut. Every so often Qunaaq lagged far behind, and Kunuunnguaq would have to wait for him. At one point Kunuunnguaq dared to ask Qunaaq; "How come you let us wait for you all the time?" inferring that he was holding them up. "I am not in a hurry was the only answer he got. But when Kunuunnguaq kept coming up with sarcastic remarks, Qunaaq got irritated and challenged Kunuunnguaq to a race.

13 Jule "Kunâk" Johs Filimonsen. Lokusimavok Tu-
nungasotmio lusámasak landstädimut ilau-
sorlâsarsimasok. Petarssûp ikingutâ.
              imänängitsok una nalerkuterugtora-
me lugluasarsimakaok upernagsákuldlo pavane
ûlumik agorsorlatlotssûsimavardlune. kingmê o-
rilätûsimáput nakússat ilimalälekarsimavordle
"ilänigok Sisimiuliardlutite autdlatamik kunák
kunúnguagkut kinguarpatdlâtâgat utarkisardlugo iläne tikiulilerssok apetâsoktaima utarkisigtarpitigutlsûkä-
nerardlugo) nukingutigsakángínama, akisimavok kunû-
ngûp akisaleriatmane kisame kämalerdlune sûkani-
ugku masimavâ arkuterkängitsukôrdlune. ânngmeta-
rikame kunúnguagkut autdlarterugtortut. Ilgdleperssarmi-
rôk piletiagdlatamik kunâpkavse tilo kalarerdlugit"

Knud Rasmussen (Kunurnnguaq) accepted Qunaaq's challenge and gave the signal he used for polar bear hunts to his dogs. He set a pace that Peter Freuchen and the others hardly could follow. While they were all driving on the ice, Qunaaq drove on land. Their destination was a hunting hut at the end of a large lake called Nassuttuup Tasersua.

When they finally neared the hut, it was easy to see because smoke was coming out of the chimney. When they arrived Qunaaq came out of the hut with steaming hot coffee and tea and said: "Have something warm."

For a change, Qunaaq was very silent that evening. And Knud Rasmussen never challenged Qunaaq again.

(takordlúgáinak)

Th. Fr.

Kunâp sugkaniugkumagdlartialik Knud Rasmussen·
nanorssiungmik kalerigînakack Pîtarssuagkut angú-
mánianartilerdlugit sujuletssorai, uvfâ Kunâk nu-
nákôrsuttorsimasukagssak. "Kaussap inâla akianîporto-
kerligsat itiodlerssuak

Th. Frederiksen,

Nâgssugtôrp "igdlukasia nuilerriatdlaramiuk pujôrssua ajorni·
anigtordlo Kunâk anilerriatdlarame kavlisorfsik titortigdlo
isáleterdlugit laimame isuma katigêtêrsimagamik "ât kavfi·
sordlulitdlo litorniarit,

        ánungiatek "laména kisame Kunâk okagsângi·
tsorssûvok kingetnalugôk Knud Rasmussínip sukánerat·
tringsila".

                Thomas Frederiksen

Qaasarsuaq was a famous rich hunter, who had made his fortune by trading with the whalers.

Here you see a whaling ship in harbour a little north of Kangiusaq. The women are wearing their national costumes and, in fine summer weather, there is a dance and the Eskimos are showing their skill at overturning kayaks and righting them again. Some whalers are swimming around near the beach to show how good they are. And some children, near where the nets were drying, try to imitate the dancers. Beside the two earth huts and tents, a women's boat is on a rack.

Kâsatssúngôx tássa pisúngorsaitai arfangniat tar‑
sivigisardlagit

ajuko arfangniat nunalisimârtut Nagsugtúp
avangnâtungâne Kangiussap erkâne arnartait ka‑
tagdlisêrtut sila alianaekisox narssánguame kitâ‑
lut kaláldlit angutitait kingusakâtaotlut arfangni‑
at ilait naluglut mêrnat ilait ikait erkâne kitilúsar‑
tut umiax napasersimasox ikâne igdlúnguit igsu‑
inait mardluk huxait ámit mardluk.

(Kalipangauvdlune kusanarnerusínaaver
tássa takorsdlúgáinarmik akerdlússamik titartunga‑
ta:

Thomas Frederiksen Iginiarfik
kâssardax tagpigerdlune toxorsimavox ivaluasárinaneta
jox kivinuxnuigutounmik pisersxuarmik Stavermut au
vanardluxne Kangexmik Kánap imâ ne iluxean se maxat.

8 August 1961

When there is not enough cod amongst the reefs where we usually fish, we go further out to the fishing banks. The cod is usually larger there, and so we can fill the boats faster. There is never any problem in finding shoals of cod, since the seabirds that feed wherever the cod feed always reveal where the shoals are.

Yesterday in a heavy fog we started out from Kangaatsiaq. This morning I was awakened by a lot of shouting and noise, and when I came out of the cabin, I saw we were surrounded by a lot of dorys. They were manned by Portuguese, who had just left their mother ship to fish from their small rowboats. The fog lifted and further out there were many ships. Outside the Uummannaq Island there were many foreign ships; from Norway, the Faroes, Portugal, Finland, France, Italy and Germany. Some were trawling, others fishing with long lines.

8 august 1961 Ikardloe sarugdlukaraluartoe akut-
dlarâgata avangmut aulisariartarpugut ilâaner-
ssuarne sarugdlît agimerusarmata, uligteârlertor-
narnerusarmat. sualingmile malamut ker-
nertumile tunugdlît agdlotartartut nalunae-
utaussarput atait sarugdlukartakigamile pu-
torugtorssuit sarugdlît nerisait agdlotarpijsa-
ramile.
        uligteârtajârdluta igpagssuc Kangâtsiamile
autdlarata uvdlât torduluåstarpalugssuarmile
iterellunga ameriatdlarama umiaussarpavssut
alcornânut pisimavdluta Portugâlimuit umi-
arssuit umiaussartatile arcâtiterdllugit tamau-
lea avalagâtdlartut pujuessimavoro avaterput-
dle umiarssuararaoro. Umânap siorâne ileâ-
nerssuit aulisartorpavssuit najortarpait. Norst-
savalingmut Portugâlimiut Finlandimiut Franslcit
Italiamuit Tysleitdlo ilait calurtut ilait nigigta-
garssertut. alisâtoimarssortutdlo.
                            Thomas Frederiksen

30 August 1961

There still is a lot of cod. The weather is beautiful, and while we were enjoying the fishing, two fishing boats "Lennert" and "Larsina" from Holsteinborg came alongside us. It is pleasant to sail side by side on such a fine calm sea. When the completely red sun set on the horizon, it was indescribably beautiful. A little later we spotted a ship burning just outside Attu. The heavy smoke created a black wall in front of the Uummannaq Island. Since lots of ships had already gone to the aid of the burning ship, we were of no help, and so we sailed back to the fishing bank. There were so many cod there that the bank felt "soft." In such fine weather we were able to sleep overnight on the open sea.

30 August 1961 15.42

sule sârugdlîwawawe 29.-ne ajianaakeissoe auli-
satdlula nuakerssiserúterdtago "Lennarth" tikiute-
riarame saneramiliúpâtigut Sissimiermiut "Pârsi-
nailiut ilagalugit tingmulkaráta núnúne sucinne
agpalugtúinâvdlune tarsilerame aliatornawawe
sunauvfa áma umiarssuak ikiuatdlagtoc

uvellálut autdllarúta pujorssuak iqssordlu-
ne Umánap siótáne (Igtup avatâne) avang-
nukaráta avangnánile onigdluge kamigdluga-
luardlugulu umiarssúp avdlap najormago ti-
mukáinarpugut Ikánermut pilwatdllaráta
kanga návánguarse sârugdlit alianaircing-
mat úmivugut.

Fisker Thomas Frederiksen
Igdmiarfik
pr Egedesminde
Grønland.

February 1962

In the month of February I was called by the school inspector, and I spent a month in Aasiaat (Egedesminde).

At the nightschool, I had opportunity to learn a little Danish, and I was very busy, since many people wanted to buy my paintings.

Here you can see the savings bank and the shipyard, where several boats have been hauled up. The towns boat repair yards are of great help to those who go hunting and fishing.

The man on the road is on his way to get ready for a hunting trip. Because of the cold weather, he is warmly dressed.

90

1962. ukiúmerane Februarime Susialiaynunga Kam-
nerijp aggeueriarmanja. váumatelle nãmátiu-
ellugo Susianjnúrdlunga, ikavalunátut unginsse-
lúrdlunga. ninautine natsumile angørssortarú-
lulerdluta, úma akúmagtúnjslanga ikalpragka-
nik giumasseraweinjmat.

Sássa Susianjne Landskassip unmatsialior-
finjua pujortulinéunk amorssersnawisor ukúi-
nerane válanjaukfiup nangminersortutelle au-
lisartut angatdllatait, ungatáne Gæstehjuinme
erijue, silútirsimasordlé sássa Handilijp unmas-
mārā nutãe "Sydder„.

unfa auna Politor Hetgo insulasiunjmat
ørsrsarsrmaualune senlarunjitunik aujalá-
niardlune autellariartortor igdllorasfit agunerit unni-
atsialiorfineardlutit ilinakiga. Thomas Frederiksen
me Susioit unniatsialiosfiunessut agssugdlaruwerit – juí-
tiliginarannik sunnernatune narssuatiataiaramik –

During my stay at Egedesminde, I came across a legend about a boy called Kaassassuk, which means "Foxtrap," and I was inspired to draw him. The children in the hamlet are teasing Kaassassuk who is an orphan. Luckily his stepmother waving her kamiut, which is used to soften boots, is coming to punish the boys and girls who are taking turns at tormenting him.

Thomas Frederiksen   Kagssagssuk

Auviangnitivdlunga "Kagssagssup putdlatuar-
figisimassâ ranigdlivaralo Aitartarsinierpâra
tâmuganar   Aâssa Kâgssagssuk mêrakatarsa
pâmissârât ikatigaluga ilarsuit sernigirugssa-
kartângimata alitusivdlingo. sernigiugivara-
porilti Aâssa arnarsiarssua igalermiorssuar, ka-
nyirmile unyiiterdinie aygertore, niviarsiarkat
pierâgagssite nuluagiarkat sâssutardlugo. kumatile ikâ-
mitingikâgamitêik sôr- Thomas Frederiksen
dle mâssârinl örinteuas-
mitut: pimartungorâgamigdle   (Aitarsagau nr 51.)
ângisungordlutik ikiorationgitarput tamâkulo mi-
tatigitengiortagkatik ikiungusinvduartarsimavait
pitorigissonssungortarsimangmata. ingminut ilu-
atiginatik ikiumalerâgata pimiortorssuartut upariu-
isutatdlu. ingmingminin issunsigimatik pigisangigalet

Once Kaassassuk heard people talking about "The Spirit of Force." So he started calling out for the spirit. And at last the spirit appeared in the form of a large fox with a long tail. "Take hold of my tail" the fox said and started to throw the boy around with such a force that all his toys fell out of his pockets. He again grasped the fox's tail and was dragged along the ground and fell over. But the third time, he landed standing. "You are now ready," said the fox and disappeared. To test his strength, Kaassassuk tried lifting a big rock and discovered he could lift the rock without even feeling the weight.

Kâgsagssuk susâmalerame nakuarssuavartartorô* si-
mut, mâgânar tordlutârtaleriarmat tikiutilieri
atdlarnerame "pissaup inua" teriangniac pamiorxot-
tôrsuac tikiutdlumilugôc ocacac pamiuma nûa-
tigut tigunga. kâgsagssup aulamugleamiuk ninic-
tisinardlune iparâtâgamigôc cangagôc pinguai sâ-
nibut auláuiq. kâgsa agdluírcutitit, ocariardlune
teriangniac. kigutdlermiuk iparâkeminic Kâgsagssu-
kagssalo tangmilcatarame nilcukaluardlunilo or-
dlonac. punga pugssânilo "milôringnâgame tarmâg-
dlônôc pugreucatâginarpoc "Aíssa nâmalcrputit teriangniac ocariardlune laimac xinagugôc. Kâg-
sagssüp nukine nisilingniardlugit ugargâtdlugssi-
ac kineriatusugdlaramiuk cangalo tângavupâ.

Kaassassuk was now indescribably strong, without anyone at the hamlet knowing. Even though the children still taunted him, he did not defend himself.

One day the kayak hunters came back towing a huge log. After several tries to drag it up on the beach, they gave up and secured the log in the water, since the weather was calm. During the night Kaassassuk got up and went down to the beach, picked up the log, and carried it up behind the huts and stuck the log into the ground. Then he went back to sleep in his stepmother's hut.

Nobody had any idea it was Kaassassuk who had brought the log up behind the huts.

Kâgsagssuk nakuarssuangorame malugitíngilat
atdlâme sule mêravataisa mitatigissarpait i-
laisa kuigât beâgsagssuk malerûtinasdlune nâ.
mátúnguamik pâmisârtítarpoq.

ilâne puniartut tikiutiviatdllarât bealigdlu-
go kissugssuak teigssiartik amuniaraluaramiko
artoramiko sigssamut pitúmarparat silagigssor-
ssúngmat. úmarotdluariaktordle malaterame sigssamut alerssuit pitútarisai kissugssúp nug-
tupkamigit amoriardlugo erssiúpâ majukanniuk
igdlup tummanut beâjutecâ tássale únardlune ar-
narssiarssuarme ivigginik okonuserdlune (atsátdles
mássákut Maskinaleritingssak ôi mâgtuleríkssutimik)
nikaginukarnerúme artor. Thomas Frederiksen
nartokarnera âma sujuleeta nalusimángiaut ka-
nok atordlugo "okeimaitsigisok,,

In the middle of winter three polar bears came near the hamlet. The poor orphan Kaassassuk ran in to ask his stepmother if he could borrow her kammikker (boots) so he could participate in the bear hunt. His stepmother threw him one kammik and said: "Get me doghides to lie on" and when she hit him with the other one she said: "Get me bearskin I can use as blankets." Kaassassuk put on the kammiks, which were too large for him, and ran out without any weapons.

Káqraqssuk ×issugssuaæ majukaluaramiuk ma-
luqineuáuqitöæpoæ paõineuáuqõmame táuna sor-
dluqtkäu.,

uküössimalersordlle doædloæait "pungaqoaæ-
ssuuæqöæ, Káqraqssulé keamiuqnik atoæniaædtaæi-
aæcaæame aqáiuaæ iseæiaæteæpoæ putuqoæssua-
ne nuiqdlaqtäætuinait, iseæme aænaæsiaæssua-
mimut oæcaæsimavoæ "keamitik atulaædlaqba,, aæ-
naæsiaæssua leauiqdlaæame keamiuqnunilæmi-
loæá "æáqroæseæigiqa,, - "keauo?,, aiqñauilé ǟma
niluqdlaædluqulæ "keipigroæseæigiqa,, euæaæsia-
leasia leanitotlaraæme niuæu leaqæqeædluqit bea-
mikinane sílauqnut. - "sunuqdlüæit sátæoæca-
æau.,,
                                    Thomas Frederiksen.

After a short while, he passed all the hunters running after the bears, who had since climbed up on top of a large iceberg. Without hesitation, Kaassassuk climbed up after them.

Kâgsagssuk arnarssuarma kamê atordlugit a-
nguterpavssuit arnagdlune katangaramigit ilu-
karssuarmut nanut kimarnssimasut ma-
juarfigai.

Thomas Frederiksen

When Kaassassuk reached the bears, he was ready to fight.
When the first attacked, he grabbed it by the front legs
and threw it against the ice. Then he threw it down to the
hunters below. When the mother bear attacked, the same
thing happened to her. In a short time, all three bears were
killed and the boy had gotten the furs for his stepmother.
And the respect he got from the people who had usually
taunted him was astonishing.

Kâgsagssuk iluliarssuarmut kakigame nânu-nut
akuitigssavdlune piarêrpoq. nânup singdlup u-
pangmane tigutigaluga anarsilamiuk innuit
akornânut milorutuai. anânarssua sernigssini-
alermat âma taimarujulo anaruteriardluya
milovingssuai tamaisilo pisaralugit. amarsiarssuane kâgssarsivdlugulo iciyigssarsivdllardleu-
gulo mitatâmartaivaox tâunaicane oeujanarniar-
figitilerpox.

    kisiâne nuleagssiarârnguax neviarsiará-
nguardlo menugssuivdllugit torssumavai taima
piniarnagit, naxgnugtarssuane
milueninguitigíngskaleardllugit, Thomas Frederiksen
imagdlait amarsiarssuane nâgssarsivdlugulo eijugssa
sivâ.

27 March 1962

The weather was beautiful today, so I went for a quiet walk amongst the ice caps.

Down there at the end of Qarsaavaralik Lake which means "The lake where the babies of the rednecked puffin lives," you can see my birthplace, Iginniarfik. The sea on the far side freezes up by the middle of winter, and that is where we fish for flounders and catch seals in nets. The land at the far end is called Tuttulik the "land of the reindeers." In Qiterleq, 5 miles from here, is our winter harbour, and to the left is the trail to Qiterleq. In the ocean visible beyond many seals are caught.

27/3 - 1962. sila aliarnaqpatdlârungmat prrulivdllunge
'sâuningup karkânut, nasigpunga tássa rqolowar-
féran inúrngorfinza Igmrsarfite mrsalârtox Kârrâva-
ragdllip karkâta ungatıne, uknorgnighgat ungatıne
imax silemarpox, walralemsarpuvdllande wagmoner-
norfijmerartarpox ungatıne muna Jugtugdlip muna,
umabralisimasrarpugutdlo Katerdllerme 8 km-but us-
rganighginume rärma bungâne tássa usmuynt avar-
fut Katerdllermut. malo waignmat rangmisson Tanr-
krârrup avurtâ 7 km-hut ungarsigtigisson ukerâkut
upumaprsakutdlo unmatrialiwegisarparput. Slâ-
ngorrssan silennen aporpox upumagrsâlent uvor-
natiput wilalunqarkartaruox Sicimiormintdllo gu-
murant Igrmorfliausrarput tassarâsrungme u-
matrialisimarannib, nagsâlent wausiqun pulrarr-
put purrrartauâidlle sule ârmit aydlaytunite natuverge
dllo.
                    Thomas Frederiksen

31 March 1962

There are a few of the children in Iginniarfik, Piitannguaq (Little Peter), Gerth, Birthe, Edvarth, Kalaasi (Klaus), Timooq (Thimothaeus), Magrethe and Nukaaraq which means little brother, but can also mean little sister. This is just a small group, but all will help to build their country when they grow up.

The building is the fish warehouse in Iginniarfik, where we sell our catch from the sea. Mostly during the season, it is quickly filled up. In the winter, it stays empty.

The trail to the left leads to the hamlet of Tunungasoq "The Upside Down;" the other trail goes to the hamlet of Ikerasaarsu "The Little Street."

The children are happy, even if their daily life is not always easy. Unfortunately, city children who are better off look down on them. Understandably, the children here are always curious, but are willing to learn. They are strong and happy, and they will grow up to be an asset to their country.

Thomas Frederiksen -62

³¹/₃-1962 tássa Igminarfingme míkeat míaríar-
tut. Pétanguaq Gîdiu, Bertu, Zavartu & Kaláte Tûnir ka-
getu Nukartáuáu munartínik culísísínguisat Kamíuínguu

Igminarfingme auliságteuninguae aussaut
avatínut aulissuaraluta kímítuuígssartangaquu
sáruguluardluarsídlugu imarautu nártaruue u-
kiumik atomuu ajorpoq piniarnerusaravtu -

uugatáue kimugsit ámítaut sámídlut
Tunumgaáuliat kagsuuut auliaríatdlo amatíp-
sarpait kímutearfordlo Igdlurmernt amunme-
rát Kardlunguit piúlíuuíngavtat ûua táuua
aratígísarpurput upumgpokut suukuuvdlugo
umntuaíuígísaríge míreat piudluartauut atou-
nínat suriuraluaágamígdlí-
nít ajoraluastuungdlu alu-- Thomas Frederiksen
gaugtsaífíuusuuít uukagimuarbuartarput kugíuánguu
alagunugtaramít, ílímarteuvellusuueararuunik kuarutuku
síuassauut - maagtíauísaasuuít seímaruuautigdlu

March 1962

The area here is an important place for Uvaks (Gadusuvak). They spawn early in spring under the ice, and they are caught because they make a good food supplement for the dogs.

Some dorys can be seen pulled up on the ice. In midstream where the water has not frozen, we use dorys for catching Uvaks. Since the current is very strong, the water never freezes. The hunters catch the seal from the shore, especially in the spring when the blackside seal comes here. The hunt is always very successful.

Further in, at Tasiusaq there are many eiderbirds in the winter. There is also a lot of cod wintering there.

Thomas Frederiksen

dássa Sarfâta på upernagssâkut Karsune 1942

Iginiarfíngup silatâtugâníspor ûwawartawaor
kirllugfigisamilco kingminutdlo nerisaritiv-
dlugit ikuartawingmat aulisartowartarspor unum
ivanile Kangerdllûnguwdlo silentâne umawssat a-
moricawsut eruput swalungmile nilcagmarâv-
dlune aulisadlune nuawrtawaor.

sporuatigut Iginiarfínguar autdlâniarfi-
ginuwartarspor nunamile upuwâlut âtârwit
ribunât alwngmigartawrigamilco, warfatuleusiuga-
mulo uliwumlûmit wlenuw ajorpor.

ilucilungâ Tarowrae niliwartawaor ulwâlut
swalungmile âma utciow tamât sârugdllingnile ulciwo-
Karsinauwor. kangerdllung-Thomas Frederiksen
ne augnwrtûnguilcaluanile erunorfuwatdlagtûrsimma-
gamu upurnagssâlcut âsrugdllwarpawnuwawartar-
por agisûtdlo ilciwarput.

March 1962

This is the old sleigh trail from Qiterleq to Iginniarfik. In the old days, when there was a Danish administrator, people used to come from Niagornaarsuk and Atalatsivik riding their dogsleighs and they used the same route to trade in Iginniarfik. When they were trading in blubber, it must have been heavy work, especially in deep snow, because it is a long trail. When the ice was gone, they used to carry their kayaks overland and then sail to Iginniarfik, which is 5 miles away.

When we go hunting, we usually start early in the morning before dawn, and when the weather is fine, it is very beautiful. In a snowstorm, however, it is only the dogs who can find the trail and stick to it, and they make sure we don't get lost.

Thomas Frederiksen

Sissa Marsime 1962 Kiterdlineq tunganik kimagsit arnartât Igimarfingmut siorartigut âma kaidlunânik ninnartorneeavartellarnat. Niavornârsule Pilatarvile-olla pigisaralegik kavellengniartarsimágut 'Sarfarmiut', ukioue aussamilo ninnartarsimavait orsnerneavaragamik. aputeartivellugo ningarfigelugo aasunavigame ungarârtulearsingame aussamilo. Kiterdlikut Sârdlûleutdlo siniudlivtik naavigelluk aitrât tikeidarsimavât. Ikam-wor uvdlilivt nal 3 autdlartarpugut ilaue

siorjorsnave arartâlo angatdlaugtirivdlugo uvdlakut sule ianmângstrov autdlariartortarpugut kimugsimik niânertawage ilsa atorssâtivellugo pirdluglamile arara nalunarsigâgat king – Thomas Frederiksen, mit kisimike iqerdlatusinnarsaqut tangmartajârmg-ssaralnardlo pingilsörnneartarolluue

March 1962

This mountain is Nuussuup Itinnera which means "Crossover at the Peninsula." At Egedesminde, in the southern district, the land is flat without any mountains. The valleys all run towards the coast. Perhaps it was the icecap that cut the tops off all the mountains, so that only the bases were left. As elsewhere in the fall, we fish in the lakes through the ice for arctic greyling.

This is an arctic greyling from Seersinninnguaq.

Thomas Frederiksen
Marts 1962 –

Núgssup idivnerata karkâ, Ausiait eruâ-
ne karkat portusûjúngitalat nuna pulâ-
tsulaujúinauvoc kíngartatdlo avangnut kô-
vîârtûgajugdlutik sermerssuakaratdlasmat nu-
ngutigâsimagunardlutik karkearssuit mô-
ngulernângôrsimâput sermup kilíortuinersou-
aink itaisit ûna avkanisûtdle itaialernerane aulisarfiguvkar-
simâput.

Thomas Frederiksen.

Sisiminguip eraluga. nr 64

24 May 1962

During the month of May we caught 11 seals on two hunting trips to Simiutarsuaq. On the way home from the second trip, with the boat already fully loaded with meat, we saw several white whales and many more seals. Later, when the weather seemed to invite us to go hunting once again, we started from Iginniarfik towards the furtherest coastline. After reaching Attu, we continued in an increasing northern wind. I navigated towards the area, where seals are normally found. However, by now, visibility had declined and we were in the drift ice, so we were forced to remain overnight at sea. We managed to kill a single seal. But on the third day, as we drifted with the ice, we reached a large group of walruses and caught a few of them. We got them all on board, and the boat was full. Suddenly the motor stalled. We had sprung a gasket, and it was necessary to keep pushing the boat away from the drifting ice. During the morning, while we were heading towards the coast under sail, we managed to repair the engine and could continue our voyage.

At this point, we were hit by a large wave that swept a barrel of fuel overboard. A door to the storage area broke and I had to hang on to it for a long time, so we would not lose it. Just before we ran out of fuel, we reached harbour in Sisimiut. "I will be damned if I can figure out how you made it through the storm in that little boat," a friend of ours remarked as he greeted us.

27/5-1962, avatâgâsit jumiariarfigisarparqut Alaj kau-
matâgâ ugssuit sihnitarssup siorane jumiari-
arnerit mardlule 11. rârfigânut aigpagssânto siku-
nut putugâta uligtsata tingmilararanta, â-
ma kilalungararporâsit natserasolluardlumila
    Une Ipiniarfingmile imartainguit ersituk kitdlo-
sgp atollôseingmata autdlarpuqut avangmut. Igle urka-
sâlariardluga avangmut avaignerâsit sudriartuartok aka-
dlunga ugssuit nugortugâs malineessataluardluga ersingi-
leriamut tâmugânak silert onersiordlugit igerdlar-
sokissut avangmute isinu-ugut, angnvigutdle tereg-
dlungmute ivdlut gungajugsâne silane tigsuter-
dluta auverpavssuit guiddlaungâgut satdlemarâr-
dlutalo tamassa usluipavut uligtâingdluta âma tâ-
ssa ugugnatâjartagârdluta martêmerput atorinarmat
silert autlairiut lêamsivdluta ungdlôpuqut uvdlôkut
tigurtârdlunga tumut anorersnalugsâvugut rôdiôrearte-
le lagnisgumle ugugnasarianta autdlartingua puqut a-
târirdlutalo kârsingsrsvigut nilav nigurtuu kutegpurput u-
sgtalo ilaut, lârt stalo matua aserormut sulerirmaguta ove-
erisilt, ilutalo sisemumut "dja tornârsut tuma anuudertgp noe a-
arotdla, malutinssox kanors, luwge atorgirsot", tatpauestdtariteekurbut

June 1962

Around the middle of June I went for a walk along the cliffs to have a look at my beautiful birthplace, feeling very sentimental. We had just bought a shrimp cutter, and when it arrived, we would be sailing south to settle in Nuuk (Gothaab).

The store and the salt house can be seen below me and the mast of our little fishing boat can be seen beyond the salt house, and out in the bay Sakaeus' fishing boat is anchored. That boat was built at the shipyard beside the savings bank in Aasiaat.

Whenever the weather got rough, we used to move the boat over to the next bay. That made a better harbour.

Thomas Frederiksen
Igiarfik. 62

June iterikutilerssoc ūmuákut Igiμiarfingme "icar-
kame. ancsasáspunga avatáne anoriulentordluta
silsiligssūgul Igiμiarfile icatsugaucx. aliauaciisar-
tarcane táissalo igdlowarfiscae imúngotfinga ūma-
icalo naggatagussanūte icimerdlūnspara rājarmiuli-
tássugsságauta Kingmutdle nūgsugssūdluta rāja-
miut silciμat nājugásteriúngμgimautigo.

        μūmuarfile tarajorterūningμardlo crsiμut
μujortulūrarcautalo amalcanajārtartup nāμarutá avatā-
tugáne Sáleálcut μujortulūrát Rūmaū ūmsatnal.ori-
fiane sarāōc. silaμiglivdlugo táissane lcisarsimás-
tarμuμut lcisángalrsivdlingule Nūμta lcángμiatuμá-
ne táumiatuμáne lcaugerdlūūmaniingūp crūtμip lciū.
Adcigaue lcisarsficarμuμit.

                Thomas Frederiksen
                        Igiμiarfile.

2 July 1962

A couple of bigger boys and myself are on our way to check our nets. We are doing an experiment with nets. At Tununngasoq the result was the best, except for too many small cod in the meshes. I was told that there used to be lots of cod in Ataneq Fjord in 1921, so we were hoping to find an area in the Fjord rich with cod.

A serious epidemic of measles had sprung up in Iginniartik. I was one of the first to get ill, and had just recovered, so I was sailing alone with the two boys. It was our hope that our fishing investigation could be continued and could protect the local fisherman from the competition of the foreign fishermen. And at several places there is an abundance of cod and flounders.

Thomas Frederiksen. 64

2. Jule 1962. nr 64.

imisugtuarsanik ilalerdlunga laugârniliar-
pugut. Tunungassup iluatungânut nigigkautsigt. pi-
sakartarput atausiardlutata tons anguarput. kisiâne
sârugdleroxanoxe. icularnângitsumigdle wangatut 1921. oi-
kutut sârugdliligssugaluarune laugerdlut stanoxe pisa-
karfigssarssugaluarpox iluamigdle misiligardlugo ilima-
narfoxaraluaxax. laungârut 400 kg angusimavait Igpiarfingme
masingmile unerasput wangale sugdlup tugellermaga
qiverdlunga katângutsilea uningmata, ularaltorsar-
put ilalindlugo táiso Ikatsigôrtugut. Tununganssup
laungârut icularnângitsunik ungaxgorssunugtsumos-
dloxine sârugdlivarpe. Thomas Frederiksen.
kaligisaroxax aulisartorssuit igain mânalisexingigata lea-
lotolit aulisariutinguinut imartaminut nalicauliinge-
icisonnut. axsut aulisagkanik misigesunuk igerallaydle
arunaraluarpox. natarmanarfoxaralucuxogana laugerdlung-
mile narua ooimartum sârugaliidlo igerdlârtaudluteli
luanik, misigassone nagisagisauaysxanax.

We have tied the boat to the nets; with the little dory we pass through an opening in the nets, and start to pull the rope ends together. That's the way to close up the nets. After that, the nets are carefully hauled by the dory towards the fishing boat; then, with a landing net, the fish are loaded aboard.

Thomas Frederiksen. 62.

bungârnit pituguvfigerardlugit. umiussamik i-
sâriaisa pitawutâ tigoriardlugo angutit mardlut
agalunaussak issâriaisa narkîmit igdlugiâgmik au-
lajagersimassoo amârtarpaut. sârac miliydlugit
tauvalo vagvudit atuardllugit umiussamut înui-
teriardlugit nâteartitajârdlugit ilustujai unniylume-
vissârdlugit aulisaghat amarunaqit puyortuliâae va-
ngdliartuârtevdllugo aulisaglat undentiartertaqut va-
lôriârnaojxxdlutik

nr 69.

Bendgârnit

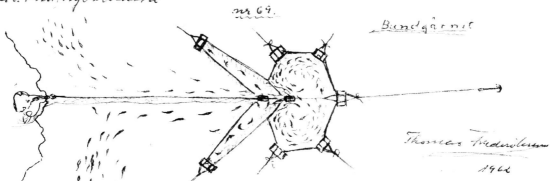

Thomas Frederiksen

1962

24 July 1962

This is the "Jorgen Peter," a 42-foot shrimp cutter, built for us at Holbaek shipyard. At the beginning of July, while my brother was still ill with the measles, I travelled to Sisimiut from Aasiaat, with other fishermen, who were also picking up their new cutters.

As we arrived, so did the cargo ship "Belles," with 20 fishing boats and two motorboats on board. Our new fishing boat is well built. It has only one fault: there is no radio on board. A couple of days later my big brother arrived, having gotten well after the measles.

On the evening of July 24th, we started out with the Hundested engine-factory director and his wife as passengers. We were very happy with our new fishing boat, which is very easy to sail. The motor is 90-100 h.p. We followed "Tuma" 36 ft. from Kangerluk near Godhavn. The next morning, in beautiful weather, we arrived at Iginniarfik.

We heard later that the cargo ship "Belles" had broken in half and was lost in the sea.

It is our hope that the fishing will improve in Greenland.

Thomas Fredriksen

24 Jule 1962. "Jørgen Peter,, GR. 9-74, 42 fods fra Hellbæk. nr 64

Jule autdlartilârtar maslengimik katángutika nâ-
parsimalerssut. Pinianqmut autdlarpunga Diskø, mut-
dle ilairdlanga Sisimiuliardluta pujortulersarnugssisser-
tut avangnâmut sqarasigalugit. Sisimiunilerssuget
umarssuarssuan "Belles,, tikerpan tájarniutit 20 mit aulisa-
dengauvan ajorutigâle jádereronjimane sumagelle-
terpigaluarptg avatisortengtpsreinangimata.

24 ne umiagtut autdlarpugut Hunested-ip Piseh-
sprea muiale ilagalugit angajuma maslingeurane
maliktaminga, tájarniut kisanaipan auglemninan
eleunile Hunested-mik motórersarpon 90-110 hlle, mele
sålerotegsauelangmile. Ikâtset hungârnu avangni-
tut dulceramaidlanga auorisânguan arellagut Thi-
ma,, Kangerdlungmut utan sarautipit uidtileut 7-
ginarpingmut ipupuget akanate.

ajoraluatinugdle Belles kragtut mine ajertisinnian lengndlugu a
nan umairunat. sper 'ita katitdlit ikarian inan.

July 1962

Towards the end of July we changed our fishing gear to trawl fishing and started to fish for shrimp in the Bay of Disko. For the first three days there, we had an instructor along. The very first time we pulled the trawl ourselves, we didn't catch one shrimp! But after that it got better and better, and we also learned several safety rules.

We usually start early in the morning, and when we reach the shrimp banks, we start first with lowering the trawl in the water and after that, one at a time, the two large and heavy "gliders" that are tied 40 yards apart on the trawl. It is these two large "gliders" that force the trawl down to the bottom of the sea, and they also keep the net open. When the trawl is lowered, one has to sail very slowly, otherwise the "gliders" will not function properly.

124

Thomas Frederiksen, 62.

1962 Jule nâlêrssoe Diskobugtimut râjarmariartoc
puget sipiligut ungugtagarssúfit susiangne pûsteriar-
dlugit. uvdlut pingasset ajoressartewariardluta nâ-
minilerpugut kaluseriarkârpiaráta susâspugut muardluit
igdlarn. pisaucartalerriardorsdlertale, âma misâlstiqut Sas-
karmiut miventarsimajut (vâjamik niventar) âma kalui-
armartoscarame sigssuernaoaor.

        uvdlâgssâlut autdlarâgavta salônfigisavta nâ-
luâ nagdluriardlugo umigdluta kalut nâlserti tarpavut sâs-
dlisartordlo sipigdlerse sungilârseinardlugo båâjagdlâkiartor-
tarpugut kalut puertivdligit. sangmivigssavtimut sâkâ-
gâta kalut kalirúnginarane svo (agdlunaussartox) nermu-
ssâsiardlugo imussac 40 favn. nâlserti tarpârput igerdlar-
nalo agdlivdlugo sârdlisârdor sijordluc nigerúsârdlugo
avalagsiânartortarpor umiatsiamik, arcordlec agdlimau-
ssartâ sulealerpat âma insamut tugdigdluyulo ni-
gisinec autdlartitarpoc sâgdlisârtutdlo nigm. tut su-
mysutigitaramik kugssagdlagable 400 favn angusarpaut
suleanârtinagit nugnive autdlarâcâmut.   Thom eg Frederiksen.
                        ...lesle na 70.

14 September 1962

The shrimp trading is done at Qasigiannguit. Here we are seen trawling for shrimps at Upernavik. Upernavik is so named because its navigation mark is the little island called Upernavik.

When the trawl is being pulled one should not change direction, nor should the boats sail too close to one another. If one gets outside the shrimp area it is possible to ruin the trawl on the rough seabed. If the trawl gets caught on the sea-bottom this is noticeable by the strain on the steel wires that attach the trawl to the boat. In that case, one stops the boat and pulls the trawl up very carefully.

It is not always possible to sell our catch, and so we are forced to throw some of the catch out.

14 Sebtember tássa 1962 me vájarmat Kasingranguanut tulássusartut, kalörfit ardlalujut uvane Upernavingme kalörpugut nalerá tássa serkarimat mardlule akornánut kuertanguac nalerauullugo Uperna-
vingmik atilik igdluartërtinane uulusarfrungdcase ujarangnartoxarame sigssuerkuatanauartarpoc u-
ma kalörtut avdlat napuumanagit kasingmas-
pat dlástariakángtdlat kalutdllo agutulerágamik na-
lunarnec ajorput vijent nalerxatgikunardlutile u-
kiluiartulersaramik nagisöxámile unuatuac uni-
tarpoc kalutdlla suumissainggata annuapatdllagtu-
viakardlune, sarpuriardllego tálast vájarimile noxisimit
ungruta uurtamik pivallertaxtimardlugit kalut kulägör-
sördlugit amörtarjuqut koxjagellina tersárdlime agu-
ngineusarpoc misterile rälextutsgpatdllimagt-
ajoralruartumagale kijet kigdleutsxaxsaxqut uulusánjmas. Th. Fr
umarsinarururmigdle kaligdlune anneunileglarpoc kvalerugssume

When the trawl is being pulled in, someone always has to stand by the winch that pulls it up, because as soon as the "gliders" surface, the motor has to be stopped. Then we sail around, so the trawl net floats up to the surface. After that the "arms" of the trawl are pulled up until the catch is concentrated in the "bag," which is then tied with strong rope and hauled on board. On the way to the harbour, the catch is sorted.

Besides shrimps, flounder is also traded, but not redfish. We were getting 7 cents a pound, but now, in November, only 6 cents.

nr. 72. inulerâgat amoxxa tarpuqut sârdlisâxtut aki-
mâningxâxnut xinxata xulâtâtâ pâxxxilxdlxgo. alximi-
Autdlo xxxigtigdlxgot xxpilâ xulâtâtâx xulxatxdlxgo itxxitxxtx
xxxgdlxgo atoxxnaxxxinxxxxxxxxx sârdli sâxtxx akimxxxxxxxx
amâxxxiaxxxx taxxâmxx. — xxxx xâxaxx lxitoxxxdl. — sârdlisâxtxt
apxilixâgata lxâjatxdlâlxxiaxtoxdlxta xalxt xxjdlxlxaxtitxxpoxxxt xgdlx-
naxxxxtâlx axxxaxdlxgo xalxt talxxa xxxx apxixixata xâjat-
dlâlxxiaxdlxxx axxajaxxx xxaxxaxxxpatxdlxâxxjxpata xgxxxxxlxxxâ-
xxx xxxxaxdlxxxx xtxxiaxtixdlxgo xxpxxxxxxxxxxxxxxxx xalxt
xxgxxxxxdlxgxt txlx axxxxxtxxpaxxxt. alxxaxxxxxlxxxx xaxxitxxax xx
xxt axxigdlxgxt xaxxitxxpxgxt xxpilxxxx. txxxxa alxxxxâxxx tx-
xxxx xxlxxxxxtxxxâxxxx apxxtxxxâxxx. xtxxxxxxâxxxpxxxxxxx.
pxxxit xxxxxxx. xxpxxxxaxxxt xâjax lxxx-xxxt xlxxxxxxxxxxxxx-
xxxâxxxt. xxâxâlxxtxdlx o/oo·xxx ÷ nxlx? xxxxxxxx
xxlxxpâxlxxxxxxxx xxxxxxx xxxxxxâxxxxxxxx

xmâlxxxxxx?

Isxxx Thomas Fxedxxixxxx

1962

November 1962

While I was out shrimp fishing, an offer to send me to high school arrived from the ministry of Greenland. Even though I was concerned for my family, I went to Sisimiut to be amongst the first people to attend Knud Rasmussen's high school.

When we were all gathered, there were 29 of us, happy and hopeful young people from various hamlets. We were the hope for the future, and it was our hope that this high school would strengthen the people and provide leadership for every new stage in the development of our country.

I am very happy with my stay. I take many notes, draw and paint, and my paintings are much sought after. With great difficulty I painted a portrait of Knud Rasmussen, which the pupils donated to the high school.

To my great pleasure, my brothers are spending the winter here in the open water town of Sisimiut.

1962-63 - Nov - *[signature]*

Knud Rasmussen Højskolen
i Holsteinsborg. *[initials]*

nr. 73 Sisimiune Højskoliaa ukiivfigigisaqarnago 1962-
me aussalut rajarnut anodlugo atorxarfigsiormatdlurit
Aakuniangilara. rajarniartugut Ministiriamik norxarfip-
nexaniararma højskolinnilearxuodllunga ilaglea isunnaqucalu-
optdlo uluunerae ilimartumit syingdlurnut rlajartordlu-
nga (atorfitgdut angalasimaneqínarma) Dais, imut iluvella
nga Sisimiuliarpunga. ilimaxatigqraslea Rusiániko Dais-
leo, mut ilasimassut inortorakil

Sássalo ilimiarbut uxuuodluta sueriqramuik tamarmik imisuytocakit ilimaqauxarmugtut ilaglugit un-
unecaore. Sássamet munarta sunqssine sumaodlitum-
gut kanoxtordlo tauna ilimiarfik sqmigrame imnu-
oxatiginut naluxaqsrotagile mutut naluxartoxtarpao-
ssornut mulixtdlasitaxumagst.

ilimiarara munaura anqanxxaardlo ilaglea ä-
na Sisimiune ukigarnite "anqukitodluxkyarnaxigame
ilisimatorssuarnik, agsut agdlagtusarmaodllugato titartajnt
klagtoxpunga ánu ualipaqkanilo prunassocarturaome tan-
kisime nagdlunqmartox Knud Rasmussen, ualipagkaxko.

Knud Rasmussen was of Greenland and Danish parentage. His body and soul belonged to Greenland. It is almost as though he is encouraging us to achieve our goals just like he did.

nr.76 74 Knud Rasmussen, angut kalâtdli-
nik ╳ sujunissalik kalâtdli.utdlo timilik a-
nersâligdlo uparissuvsulut ipoн anguniaka-
nut ínpmassut nikatdlujuitsôruvdluta.

Early Part of 1963

There is a beautiful view from the Church Hill towards the Kaellingehaetten, a highly characteristic peak in Holsteinborg. Knud Rasmussen's high school is located just below this peak. During my stay at the high school we had lectures from 8 a.m. to 12, and again in the afternoon and, as a rule, also in the evening. It could be very difficult to sit still that long, especially if you were a hunter.

The fall weather has been changing a lot, first thaw, then frost and then storms. After the New Year the weather becomes more stable, with a nice strong cold front.

nr. 76

1963,p auteilartinerane Sisimiune ukiore oealugfiup sa-
manik leangimut waeaennae "Vacannæe", "Kglengehatten",
alutornartuaue sualeniginile ieaneok. tornerniudleue
hfseol.niudllata tõnunume eaneap etiunile silageriue-
taeingut ... uellahat aefimae pingannunile uelleip eeneamit
maedlunile aefnernut. aefimae pingannudllo eeneamit i-
nuleut iline eulailuap euea roeaetaeingut anyalietuae.
toenunavdleue toeneenunue iponanenue etingreeajania-
leungtaeungelae.
        ueaeuartoenerane sila ueeaisimangenaoe iisaep-
aetaellune auoeeueueiaetaedlunile. Ute.oeki.éemutdle Hfjeleo-
ganile tapiliangap nepioetaegpaetigut.

                                    Thomas Frederiksen

        ....
        .... raeue aeguroe ealeeuneunuevelue

18 March 1963

While I still was at the high school, the sea started to freeze, to great bother for the shipping. My brothers were often out, and usually came back with a good catch. One day we heard a radio distress signal from "Benedicte," which was in trouble in the drift ice. When they came home, the captain told us that he had seen my brothers out on the sea with a good catch. March 14 was very cold, and the sea started to freeze up, and furthermore a strong north wind prevailed along the coast. I started to worry, and began to ask when they were last seen. On March 15 I asked the police to start a search. But because of poor weather conditions, no planes could be used. The police cutter went out several times, but turned back due to very poor weather. The north wind was pushing the drift ice towards the south. My anxiety grew, and I did not dare to tell my parents. Finally a trawler "Qerrortusoq" had seen them far out from Itelleq. "Jorgen Peter's" screw had been damaged by the ice, and they were drifting with the floes. March 18 I got a message that "Erica Dan," on the way to Sisimiut, had gone to their rescue. At the same time "Ilik" went out and came back the same evening with "Jorgen Peter" in tow. They had caught 1 white whale, 6 walruses and several seals.

From now on, cutters of this size should always be equipped with radios for emergencies.

136

ᐃᓪᓚᑦ ᓄ ᐁ. 18 Marts 1963. højskolerme psuserustulartunga siku-
martorsusingorpoc iláka avangmut puuariartarput pusa-
kartaodlutigdlo. 8 Marts iláka autdlaruimajuut 12 Marts sikumar-
torssuángorpoc angalaunut alurantisusumik aydlugtorsábugar-
mauisdlo "Berutekta, silume ajornartorsurpalugpor rádeovarame
ibluikamik ilagla takusuimauollugit ocarput pusuarstariruinaout
14.marc silungalugtuimarpoc sonaugarme avatálunit avá-
ngangtorsuivdlume. sumválulurame páuimargavla sume lagua-
dlumé taluneararmumersuut, 13 Marts Politiunit kalarimunya ke-
nermrealermuvdllugit tingimsartumugdllunit tingmisartouolle
autdlarsimausimángilaue sela yocunymut Politikdllo ungatdla-
tat "Ilik, autdlartaralisarpoc uterdllunik summunisit avatá du-
kumisut avángangtorame kulanuangisumik silut kujang-
muticsámutausit kujangmut avangmut talumurame sugto-
kalarupunga ilávdllunga. atátálusimitdlo nalunássamut opules-
dlunga rusimáluranga. Enme pumariat "Konurtusaákut Jágdllup a-
vatóne avasiguau me nauimatorsimavait "Jógen Péter, sarpiarsumm-
dlume tissutuartore. 18 Marts "Rebeka Dau "ip arcuuárdllugo kuuar-
tará tealurigpauga silaniigdlo userortunvdllugo Ilunp kaligluuoru
toraminuk uinilusore briejput ulalungau luufisit t upsugule pusuusumuc-
dllugit, sasunik busaum poru "rádnelgogrungitust ráduluruuriando-
upt rádhedugavuutait mungsurugamudle.
  1 Marts ...... taunt, taume ogtijuvou tálulularmumuvolua

16 March 1963

This boat is probably the last of its kind in West Greenland.
It belongs to Otto Petersen of Aalatsivik. On our way to
Niagornaarsuk with the area administrator we landed
at Aalatsivik, a hamlet that used to be heavy populated
because of the rich hunting. However, now only one
family lives there. In the winter they catch seals. In the
spring when the ice breaks up, they go fishing in Arfersiorfik-
fjord and later hunting reindeers. Recently they have found
a place where there is plenty of flounder. And there are lots
of eiderbirds all winter. Flounder and eiderbirds are a
good source of income in the winter, when they can be
sold in Egedesminde. Otto Petersen, who is known as "Big
Otto," is a competent and careful hunter.

billede nr. 70/16 Maj 1963. Aulatsivingme Otte Petersen ip
erinâ. Igsiarfingmik innersiarput Lars Osterman
ilagaluga atåtskutdle Kaurnärssulersarput imitut.
dle aulatsivingmut siornagut itserdle puisiarfigigssot.
ssigame inorsardluarsimagaluartumut massåkut.
dle igdle ataussinångortume nagsgalik umiarcar-
ptor kularnårngitsumik kitâne umiat itsoe sigular-
ta agatdlatitorqaisa atortut laigutdllersât uleirme
puisimåsarput anssamilo Pepersiarfingmut ersalang-
niardllatigdle anunariartarsimåput. massåkutdlo an-
latsiviup ersâne katersisarfile puisardluartos nag-
ssårinuarsimavoe. åna Sarfap ersâ uleirme ini-
tiligssisarpoé Susiangmutdlo nersisarivdluastarpait
Kiaurnarssungmut tunisisararnik. Osterupis puniartut par-
ssigesartui
sligsit.

                                          Thomas Frederiksen.

25 October 1963

Towards evening I went for a walk over the cliffs at Ilulissat, also called Jacobs Havn, and looked at the majestic mountains over by Sermermiut Bay. I was gazing towards the sea to the south and started to think of a poem about Jacobs Havn by Otto Rosing: "Oh I am so happy to be in Ilulissat"...

Two kayaks are coming in, they have most likely been bird-hunting, and it is said that there are many seals around here. The ruins nearby show that it has been inhabited for many years. Out there in front of the gigantic icebergs is where we used to catch shrimp. However, ice in the sea can interfere with the trawl fishing. Now and then, in between the ice floes we can spot seals. Nearer the coast is where cod and flounder are caught.

Sermermiut.

25 ne Oktober 1963 Ilulisat sarsärmit Iuspunga úmgi
atuluissoa ilulianumikalg wirmullördlugit kutamak-
sut tássa ~~Sermermiut~~ avangnut kujangnut sa-
wurunga oúmiwsitalu kersit exsävan "lí Ilulissat
mandusdatea, wärsat madlule ilungmukärput mu-
termarmardlubile ama pusuwastarmamawax sirma-
gane Ilulissure rüjamerpuget kaursumilo kager-
dlüp Ilulissat bangerdluata avatäne ratörtarfu-
gut ilulianavsmut Armilralugit ke sime ilula
mumerparsmut xwanilunjutarput sudlunge mle
tastmue sikurornartawal ss li akornule pusewarla.
simawait ämalo Fisher Thomas kederselsen.
sárugdluearfewarpos.
ralvsligmrsemawadlimilo.

When I went back, I stood above our hamlet and looked at the icebergs slowly drifting by. I could not help thinking that the hunting and fishing are ideal here. Through the ages people admired the spectacle of the big icebergs, but also have been scared of the force with which they come crashing down. Spectacular but awesome when they crash. It is said that when in a kayak, one can hear sounds just before an iceberg crashes, and so one can escape.

nr. 78 billede

iglukoxarfigdlo alagkaraka avangmut iluliarssuit
amiartorusärtut avaleralugit takordlilerpavka sijule-
vut kanox nerriguqtängitsigigssanerssut akianä-
mudlutigdlo ämale kularnángitsoumik iläne
kuilertämisimasnartángitsörunángilax tässame
iluliarssuit iläne aserortaqssagamik kusanaralu-
aralutik amilämisimanangitsörnex ajoramik a-
serulegkusugdlaraqamik kisiäne aserormaleräqamik
kajartotdlune nalunarnex ajosumäput imap ilua-
tigut nutälornere malurigmartarsimagamik ku-
mänigssarnut pirfigssaxarnartarsimavox

Titler   Thomas Frederiksen
          Ple Jørgen Peter,

Our forefather's existence was based on hunting and fishing. Human beings are cruel; when the prey is dying in pain, they are happy; but if the animal escapes, they are upset.

There are many reindeer in our country. In the old days they were hunted with bow and arrow. But having to carry the dead reindeer on your back was the worst part of reindeer hunts. When the tame reindeer were brought into the country, they brought some diseases with them, and this infected the skins of the wild reindeer. Nature controls the numbers of reindeer. They thrive best in the green areas. They are very beautiful animals. Nowadays, they are hunted in the winter from dogsleighs.

Thomas Frederiksen

Today there are too many reindeer, and they are weak and no longer shy. In the winter herds of reindeer gather in the middle of the frozen lakes, that way they detect danger easier and can make their getaway. The bucks hide on the inaccessible cliffs.

Nowadays hunters lie in wait ahead of the reindeer when they are on the run, but it is said that in the olden days the hunters could run as fast as the reindeer.

tugtut mâna sârqitsúput, nujuarpat dlâ-
rungnâvdlutigdlo. tugtut nujuartat uкиu-
me issiterúgat tatsit ивкânut katerssûtar-
put naviânartumik tâkútor.araluarpat
sumut. "sumut! sâriarngisartik piarêsi-
gеûdlugo agisôrtarssûlo tikitkuminâne
rusumitarput vакanilúnit!

        kulavait sijulerssortaisarput оvila-
samaitdlo kalâtdlissûtdlo ingmikuka jâ
arpâsigdlit inugavisavsimângilait! puguq-
tait naisardlugit ;pugsuvagtârdlutit âma
simagdlutik,, e puilaunigdlagtârdlutigdlo ; ки-
larnaрngitsumik simagdla'tiginartagkaminik.

                Thomas Frederiksen.

When the hunters came back with a good catch, there was always lots of excitement. And everybody wanted to hear about the hunt. Sometimes the discussions got very heated, and were difficult to stop; only the drum songs were able to smooth things over.

In some of the sagas it is told that people (without the use of rockets) travelled to the moon.

The seasons were calculated by the stars.

Our forefathers' boats and kayaks are so well developed and functional that they can withstand the strongest force of nature.

pisiasiaualluardlatiqdle takikâgamik manasartarsima
kait pigssaganaitorsiortarneritdlo sôrdle adllase pi
sartor tusarumanusartarsimakait, ilámle áma nu
anârnerat sualuleriardlunik agssortûtorssuángor
tarsimáput lussäârudlutik merleruartunnik,
naggatâgutdlle ilaátitarsimáput akerunerit so
rârdlutik ardlâmik nâgkununsagamik ingmúmitdllu
mit usuarsartiudlutik kuhunnitik pusigâgamikok, su
nuvfexaratik ingmingnut ajugasfigiuartarsimagâmik
agdlâme rakeitumik atorkoxaratik seamangmuka
tarsimáput sulimi mássikut üusalaunsa, mâlagau
marta amerdlavaldlâkâgala "itermikal pusérpiliq
naussuit,
magdluisiat atorneartarsimáput iláinle akungivis
dlugit ilaátitsorsaxastarsumunsa agatdllatait tumersu
tit pissásigamik akunsagssaitdllo salkortoxalutik,

Thomas Frederiksen.

Kenertarssuar
(Godhavn)

Imerissut
(Kronprinsens Ejlande)

Disko Bugt.

Ilulissat
(Jakobshavn)

Ilimanar
(Claushavn)

Akitsigssuarssuit
(Hunde Ejlande)

Angisat
(Grønne Ejlande)

Kasingôriânguit
(Christianshåb)

Akunae

Iginniarfik

Ikamiut

Egedesminde

Ausiait

Nivâe

Manermiut

Akugdlit

Kitdlit
(Vester Ejlande)

Iginalik

Kenertalussuatsiar

Natermae

Iluliatik

Sarfarssuac

Tunerton

Afsersiorfik

Natsiorfik

Kenertaussuac

Hurdlessernerssoec

Imilissuac

Perthe strandou

Kangâtsiar

Niakornarssuk

Autatsiuik

Tupinarssuac

Ataner

Margorssuac
Aratsiak
Iginiarfik
Tugarssuac

Simiutarssuac

Igdlukoe
Igdlukassua

Tessrarae

Akia

Antyssserniae

Jalut

Ûmanar

Arpaggfik

Kitsarsut

Innajsuk

Naajat

Semiutat
Tasiusak

Ukivik

Nordre Isortoq

Saqqat

Sisimiut
(Holsteinsborg)

Aqissineutat

Amitsdoe

Sarfanguan

Kendak

Imanarsuk

Ikertak

Sarneardlit

Itivdlen
Kangerdlua

Søndre Strømfjord

Kangerdlugssuak